The Mind Field

"THE

Robert E. Ornstein

MIND FIELD

A
Personal
Essay

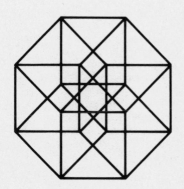

THE OCTAGON PRESS
LONDON

ISBN 0-86304–011–X

ACKNOWLEDGEMENTS:
"Where it Starts" p 49 *The Magic Monastery* © Idries Shah 1972,
Octagon Press, 1982; "The Book in Turki" p 61 *Wisdom of the
Idiots* © Idries Shah 1969, Octagon Press 1979; "Literature"
p 166 *Thinkers of the East* © Idries Shah 1971, Octagon Press
1982; "The High Knowledge" *The Way of the Sufi* © Idries Shah
1968, Octagon Press 1982; "The Tales of the Sands" p 23 *Tales of
the Dervishes* © Idries Shah 1967, Octagon Press 1982; "The
Inexplicable Life" p 155 *Tales of the Dervishes* © Idries Shah
1967, Octagon Press 1982; "The Initiation of Malik Dinar" p 148
Tales of the Dervishes © Idries Shah 1967, Octagon Press 1982;
"How and What to Understand" p 109 *Thinkers of the East* ©
Idries Shah 1971, Octagon Press 1982; "The Man Who Was Easily
Angered" p 79 *Tales of the Dervishes* © Idries Shah 1967, Octagon
Press 1982; "Appetite" p 57 *Thinkers of the East* © Idries Shah
1971, Octagon Press 1982; "Meatballs" p 191 *The Magic Monas-
tery* © Idries Shah 1972, Octagon Press 1982; "Duty" p 151 *The
Magic Monastery* © Idries Shah 1972, Octagon Press 1982;
"Contrary to Expectation" p 9 *The Book of the Book* © Idries Shah
1969, Octagon Press 1976.

(Page 143 constitutes a continuation of the copyright page.)

For Punkington,
Midgit, and Moose-Brain

Preface

We are now on the threshold of a new understanding of man and of consciousness, one which might unite the scientific, objective, external approach of Western civilization and the personal, inward disciplines of the East. The emergence of this new synthesis has caused many to flock, unthinkingly, to rudimentary spiritual sideshows, which are quick, cheap, and often flashy. These reductions have given strength to others' total lack of interest. I write to develop a more secure position, one of interested yet candid assessment, somewhere between the two dominant positions: the almost reflexive rejection of what is conventionally understood as "mysticism," by many in the "hard" areas of contemporary life; the reflexive adulation characteristic of the slavish consumers of guruism, "instant enlightenment training," and other degenerations.

I spend much of my professional career as a drudge, performing research on the function of the two hemispheres of the human brain. My colleagues and I write technical papers on spectrum analyses of electroencephalographic indications of differences in function between the two halves of the brain, and on the correlation of transient changes in brain function with cognitive performance. To support our research I worry over technical grant proposals and the construction of a laboratory, and share in the hiring and firing of personnel. And to communicate our findings I write textbooks, organize symposia, and try to keep a small interdisciplinary institute solvent.

Though I am asked constantly what I think of various developments in consciousness, since I am involved in the area, my normal academic responsibilities preclude much response. Most of those who inquire are people who are not professionally involved in the study of the mind, but who may have heard or felt something of an extended consciousness or of esoteric traditions. They have heard about meditation, or about Eastern traditions of mysticism, or about training of intuition, yet naturally they recoil from such confusions as learning Sanskrit, Arabic, or Japanese as part of a spiritual endeavor; supporting "Tibetan pen-pals"; searching for Atlantis; or joining "gourmet vegetarian societies." These people may have heard of the new discoveries about the right hemisphere of the brain, or about research in parapsychology or in the nature of the "new religions," and they may be wondering *what is in it for them*, how much of all this is relevant to their own lives.

I have attempted to write a book that is not primarily for the academic community—except as academic people might personally be interested in these areas. There is little technical or academic jargon. The book is short, its ideas and conclusions distilled. It is not a textbook but a personal essay on the results of investigations undertaken, originally, for myself. It is written in plain language for serious people, whatever their technical or professional competence in the areas of the study of consciousness.

I hope the book will prove in a small way elucidating to many who have wondered whether they should go to a psychotherapist to deal with their interest in consciousness, whether there is anything useful in "awareness training," whether they should meditate, whether they should travel to the East, whether they should seek refuge in Shamanism or in systems of thought more relevant for cultures different from ours, or more relevant perhaps for a different epoch.

I have tried to make the essay as clear and compact as possible, and I have tried not to mince any words or conclusions, in contradistinction to the normal politic manner of the textbook writer and the pedant. I also have included a few interesting designs to look at, both to convey the overall theme of the differences between the container, or the package, of this extended knowledge of man, and the content—and in some cases to assist in the communication of that content, especially to the brain's right hemisphere.

This book is based more on personal experience than any of my other books, based as it is partly on my travels in Asia, Africa, and Europe, as well as on my twelve years as a research psychologist and on my personal acquaintance with people involved in meditation, parapsychology, brain research, and connected disciplines.

Contents

The Container
and the Content

Cross and Christians, end to end, I examined them. He was not on the Cross. I went to the Hindu temple, to the ancient pagoda. In none of them was there any sign. To the uplands of Herat I went, and to Kandahar. I looked. He was not on the heights or in the lowlands. Resolutely, I went to the summit of the mountain of Kaf. There only was the dwelling of the Anqa bird. I went to the Kaaba of Mecca. He was not there. I asked about him from Avicenna. . . . I looked into my own heart. In that, his place, I saw him. He was in no other place.

Thus the poet Jallaludin Rumi of Balkh described his own search for knowledge in the literary manner acceptable seven hundred years ago. His manner of expression, rather than the essence of his thought, has been much imitated by contemporary obsessionals. Many writers confuse spirituality with a lofty metaphysical whining over the disappointments of contemporary life. One anonymous contemporary spiritual flatulent writes, "In the personal crisis of *my* life, where should I turn?" I hope not to add to the reader's worry: this book will not be more of the same otherworldly longing. Yet I begin with Rumi, primarily to emphasize the distinction between inward and outward aspects of truth.

It is an unfortunate accident of the twentieth century that those most interested in personal knowledge and in an extended conception of man tend to be those least suited to gaining or using them. The receptive investigator encounters innumerable freaky, peaky psychologies and associations, advertisements in the Sunday newspapers for courses of training in instant self-improvement, phone solicitations, "quest seminars," cults devoted to parapsychological phenomena, self-preoccupation societies in the name of Encounter, Freud, or Ouspensky, and tiresome loonies of almost every persuasion. Many people are looking for a cause or doctrine to attach themselves to, which will take them to a "new level of consciousness" through such enterprises as boarding unidentified flying objects, or through a "new development" such as next year's yellow-vegetable or all-marsupial diet for weight loss, job improvement, sexual potency, and spiritual development.

These cults and people are, simply, not an appropriate ground for anyone wishing to reintroduce a more complete understanding of man. Responsible people in the arts, sciences, business, humanities, and the professions shy away from this area because of a bad odor associated with its clannish, cult aspects. Who could fail to be repelled by a turgid metaphysicization of almost every aspect of life, one which leaves no room for ordinary joys and accomplishments; by writers who are always having their guts wrenched by one or another imagined "crisis," whether of the spirit, of business, or of the flesh? If an interest in consciousness and an extended personal understanding of life has, in our time, been the province mainly of those outside the mainstream of contemporary life, it is understandable in terms of the radical cultural changes of the twentieth century.

The superheated and explosive economic, social, and scientific growth of the past two generations has left many who have grown up in this era convinced that a world without material limits is the norm. It has, for many, been their only experience of the world. The ideals of limitless expansion have shaped our marketplace, economic planning, and social life, and they do inform the background of science and the humanities. Our politicians conventionally promise as much as is possible in the relief of the constancies of our condition; our scientific endeavor is unchecked by a traditional perspective; and our culture is the best-educated, wealthiest, most "emotionally aware" in history, and—as a concomitant perhaps—one of the most spiritually illiterate. In an era devoted primarily to decreasing death rates, improving living conditions, and developing science, there is little time left for other considerations. Yet, in spite of this progress in our material welfare and health, we do not often note that the death rate is still 100 percent.

We are, I think, at a transition point: the beginning of the end of this adolescence. In many areas people are beginning to feel that we have left something (without knowing what) out of our cultural upbringing, out of our science, medicine, education, and personal development. Perhaps we base too many of our plans on the assumption of social and material progress, an assumption rooted in the seemingly limitless growth of the past two generations.

Yet even those people who are most concerned and interested in traditional approaches to human development still attempt to judge them with the stunted perspective of a contemporary ethnocentrism. Our "no limits" culture provides the basis: The North American baseball championship for men is the "World" Series. We may be informed by our television weather announcer that the "all-time" record for rain or heat was set on a certain date: here, "all-time" usually means the past hundred years. Our medical, educational, and scientific journals rarely refer to any fact or finding published before 1940 (with the exception of an obligatory honorific reference to Greece), and anything discovered or understood before the First World War is considered ancient history. In our approach to science and to consciousness, we bear the remnants of identifying our culture's specific developments with the sum total of knowledge and we attempt to measure some of the most important traditional human ideas on the scanty yardstick of our own habits of mind.

Scientists and humanist scholars are men and women of their times and share both the benefits of our culture's developments and the blindness of our collective shortsight. Their blindness and distortions render many of our otherwise most competent and educated people unequipped to judge ideas and developments in personal knowledge. Even those who are most interested often treat personal development as a less valuable side of themselves. Ideas in that area might seem "too old," associated too much with an old-fashioned and degenerate religious mysticism, perhaps conveyed by a nut or a tramp, a person less well-socialized. We find, then, a large group of productive men and women, who might draw from and contribute to an extended understanding of human nature, closed off from it by the strengths of their cultural training—and a second group all too eager to be told that "life is an illusion" and to join up here and climb aboard the next Kosmik Union Special, flying saucer, or Guru-of-the-Month Club.

An interested observer of the middle ground is in for some considerable discomfort, since those actively pursuing several interesting ideas have been drawn a bit over the edge. Parapsychology, to the receptive mind, is an area of research which is at least worth some serious, sober, and open-minded scientific investigation. However, one sometimes finds conversations with enthusiasts in the area sliding from a reasonable discussion of a single experiment to the Bermuda Triangle, unidentified flying objects, oddball encounters, or massage techniques. People seeking "growth" find their needs for personal knowledge blunted and diverted to successful and rich institutions, with massage, sexual athletics, investment schemes, parties, incomprehensible doctrines such as those of Gurdjieff, Kahunism (a flying-saucer cult), "yoga tag," or simpleminded meditation offered as a substitute for transcendence. Such "growth centers," I fear, are to

be understood more in the sense of "growth stocks" and child-
ish self-indulgence than as anything seriously concerned with
human development.*

I attempt, in this book, to begin to separate the current
lofty metaphysical inflation, the goofiness, the outright lies, and
the commercialism, from the real possibility and discipline; to
separate the more occult extravagance from a developed and
hard knowledge about areas not represented enough in contemporary life. I hope that these and other efforts will lead
toward a new synthesis of ideas both traditional and modern,**
one which might yield a consistent development of man found
neither in the static traditional cultures of the East nor in one
so unrooted as our own.

There is an intriguing moment toward the end of the widely
disseminated television series and book, *The Ascent of Man.*
Jacob Bronowski, historian of science and ideas, after a brilliant
account of the intellectual and material development of Western
societies, sums up the "ethnocentric" position:

> And I am infinitely saddened to find myself suddenly sur-
> rounded in the west by a sense of terrible loss of nerve, a re-
> treat from knowledge into—into what? Into Zen Buddhism;
> into falsely profound questions about, Are we not really just
> animals at bottom; into extrasensory perception and mystery.
> They do not lie along the line of what we are now able to

---

* This simplemindedness is often communicated by the announcements for
these "centers." Here is a recent poem by one of the successful graduates:

A Celebration
I swim in the sun
I sail to the stars
I swing with a song
I sway with the wind
I see the sound of a sigh
I am centered
I am Sophie

Sophie
Age 32

** Or Eastern and Western.

know if we devote ourselves to it: an understanding of man himself. . . . Self-knowledge, at last bringing together the experience of the arts and the explanations of science, waits ahead of us.

Here, in a nutshell, is precisely that insular view of our intellectual and material "ascent" which has left many blinded to the specialization of different traditions—shortsight which is identical to that of the "all-time" record. In the Western scientific tradition, we transcend the limits of personal knowledge by developing the outward, "objective" sciences, whose data are available to all observers and are based upon repeatable experiments. Yet we do not understand that the vagaries of ordinary personal experience can be transcended in another way, by inward studies of the shifting personal biases themselves. In the East, those most concerned with the problems of man, life, and the mind have developed specialized exercises to defeat these continual transient shifts in personal awareness. These developments of consciousness occasion a mode of knowledge complementary to the ordered sequence of intellectual inquiry. That hundreds of years of religious inquisition and degeneration might well have formed the basis of our opinion of such "esoteric" endeavor I have no doubt, yet the rejection of the essence of religious and philosophical tradition has left a fundamental gap in our contemporary approach to reality. Disciplines and techniques of human development are beginning to return to prominence in the West, in a new form, some even divorced from their religious or cultural associations. These techniques and traditions meet unthinking rejection by some—and equally unthinking acceptance by others.

In this book I intend to explore several of the most important developments, sometimes in differing prose styles. Beginning with the reasons for our continual searches in this area, one should keep in mind another statement of Rumi: "Counterfeiters exist only because there is true gold."

2

Some Remarks on the Evolutionary Background of Consciousness

We are biologically obsolete. The most recent anthropological estimates place the appearance of man, the genus *Homo,* at least 3,750,000 years ago, the result of millennia of continual evolution to suit the alterations in conditions encountered. Many of our dominant characteristics are derived from our evolutionary basis developed long ago to adapt to conditions which no longer apply. By a most generous estimate, modern man, or *Homo sapiens,* appeared well before ten thousand years ago, at about the time of the Agricultural Revolution, sometime between what are classified as the Old and New Stone Ages. We can assume for the sake of this discussion that modern man is "only" ten thousand years old, though many of his characteristics are much, much older.

Cultural evolution is much more rapid than biological evolution. An alteration in learning or the acquisition of a skill can be transmitted quickly between individuals, or with modern means of communication transmitted to an entire culture, yet our *genetic* structure remains unchanged. Thus the biology of living systems always lags behind alterations in the environment or the social situation. Man remains basically unchanged genetically since the Stone Age.

The primary aim of physical evolution is biological survival, both of the individual and of the race. At points in the history of a large population system, individual survival may proceed along the same parameters as the survival of the population,

11

though at later points on the curve of increasing population and social complexity there is often a dissonance between them. It is in large part man's increasing mastery over his environment that cleaves the individual and collective prerequisites of survival and occasions the need for new choices, and new development.

Even restricting ourselves to the last ten thousand years, we can consider that in the early period of human evolution the survival of each individual was paramount to the survival of humanity as a race. Since we of the present generation have lived exclusively in a period of explosive population growth, we do not often fully realize that the world population was quite sparse throughout most of our evolutionary history. As late as the time of Christ, eight thousand years after the Agricultural Revolution, the total human population is estimated to have been about equal to the current population of the United States of America. In this spare and largely unordered history, personal threats from starvation, marauding animals, and natural disasters formed many of the primary obstacles to the individual's, and to humanity's, survival.

A key element in the survival and development of man has been the ability to separate diverse aspects of a situation, to analyze, to develop language and calculation, to reduce complex situations to their components, and to measure advantages in a sequential manner. A personal consciousness, if I may continue to extrapolate, based on the integrity and inviolability of the individual, could be most useful in conditions continually threatening an individual's survival. In such a situation one would need to be able to isolate threats—natural, animal, or human—in the environment. The "flight or fight" response, for example, would be of great survival value here, as would hoarding food, or overeating when a food supply became transiently available; so would producing many children, a few of whom might survive to provide for their parents.

A personal consciousness which could separate the self from others and take a strictly analytic position toward oneself and the world was, I think, a major impetus to the development of rational thought, and the achievement of a secure material and technical basis for agriculture, communication, and culture. What we normally consider the highest intellectual achievements of man are developed on the basis of analysis and a sequential mode of interaction with the world. Those who exhibit this mode of consciousness would have the advantage in a time of crisis. Consider the opposite: a person of "mystical" bent, immersed continually in the "identity of all things," one who would think "here is one of God's creatures, about to eat another of God's creatures" when a man-eating bear approached, presumably would not have much chance of contributing to our genetic heritage.

Rational analysis, although it engendered the dominion of man, has also altered the nature of man's environment. We have, through language, science, and technology, re-created the modern world we live in, yet we remain, biologically, Stone Age men and women. Although we may not be as completely hopeless as the popularizing evolutionists describe us, who attribute to man an immutable and fixed "territorial imperative," we continually pay the price of the time lag between our social and physical evolution. The interpersonal environmental and social stresses of an urban environment often call forth the adrenalin of an extreme "flight or fight" response where none is required. We face the potential of overpopulation due to our inability to decrease the birth rate in conjunction with advanced medicine and public health. And we face obesity in half the population * when food and drink are plentiful. Some writers in the medical community now recognize "diseases of civilization," which are due to the mismatch of genetic and cultural factors: overeating, especially of sugars, has deleterious effects on the heart and may contribute to diabetes; an overrefined diet may contribute to gastrointestinal cancer; the hazards of smoking and urban pollu-

---

* In some Western European countries, more than three-quarters of the population are overweight.

tion on respiration are well known. As René Dubos has pointed out, when we are injured our skin forms a scar to protect the process of healing, but in internal injuries this "wisdom of the body" is not wise but dangerous. In the liver, for instance, a scar is cirrhosis.

One cannot pass a day without reading new, technical, piecemeal solutions to these problems—everything from diet changes to improved smog devices, from increases in exercise to solar energy since these are piecemeal, secondary phenomena —yet the primary necessity now is for a reconstruction of the primary mode of human consciousness, in complement to our rational and analytic reconstruction of the nature of our world. The most pressing need of our history, that of personal, individual survival, is aided by the cultural and intellectual evolution of the past ten thousand years. The ancient and pressing human problems of an adequate supply of food, provision for shelter and for the safety of reproduction have been technically solved in advanced industrial societies. Compared with the state of the species during the bulk of our evolutionary history, relatively few people in the developed countries today are prey to starvation or natural disaster. The survival problems that we now face are much more complex, if only because they exist at an emergent level of thought and action. Our problems are collective rather than individual: the development of more and more brilliant insights on the relationship of mass to energy has inevitably involved us with the possibility of nuclear holocaust. The increasing degradation of our atmosphere has begun to threaten health and life on a large scale. Unchecked and accelerating increases in population could threaten large-scale starvation in many parts of the world.

When we deal with situations which collectively affect humanity, a focus on individual analysis and survival is of less and less value. A man may wish for many children, for instance —a wish based partly upon vestigial evolutionary predispositions —even though he may be contributing to a population imbalance on a larger scale. For a genetic solution to these problems we would have to wait too long. Edward Wilson writes regarding genetic change that there is "every justification from both genetic theory and experiments on animal species to suppose that rapid behavioral evolution is at least a possibility in man. By rapid I mean significant alteration in, say, emotional and intellectual traits within no more than ten generations—or about 300 years." This is usually considered an "optimistic" assessment.

We cannot wait for biological evolution or for new political or social programs, or, even, for new ideas. What is needed, rather, is a shift in mode of consciousness by many people away from the egocentric, individual focus toward one geared more to overall relationships between entities. Such an "emergent" consciousness could convey a more comprehensive perspective of the life and action of an individual and of a group, as well as the relationships among seemingly disparate activities and systems. It would augment the Stone Age or, at best, the "frontier-society," "me-first," "every-man-for-himself" attitudes inherent in our ordinary consciousness.

I am aware that a suggestion of such a reconstruction of human consciousness seems quite out of place in our technical society, perhaps absurd, naïve, or an example of escapism or wishful thinking. It may seem this way partly because of our culture's shortsightedness and almost complete lack of understanding and expertise in the technology of human consciousness. How many of us realize, for instance, that our ordinary world, our ordinary consciousness, is a restricted, selective *construction?* Our consciousness does not completely reflect an external reality, but only a minor sample of the flux of potential experiences. We create our personal worlds in three major ways: by our biological "design," by our shared cultural heritage, and by our own daily choices.

We normally consider that we see with our eyes, hear with our ears, smell with our nose, feel with our hands, and that impressions thus derived exhaust the nature of reality. Although this is partly true, the main biological function of our sensory systems is to discard information which is irrelevant to biological survival. Our senses are as selective as cats' whiskers; our eyes focus on a small spot within the radiant electromagnetic band, our ears respond to a narrow bandwidth of mechanical waves. Very little of the available information passes the barrier into our "known" world.

Our shared language and culture similarly limit our experience. Speakers of different languages may share a common structure of discourse and assumptions, but filter out much which is outside their own language, or world-view. There is, for instance, no proper word for "consciousness" in French. Differences among the Indo-European group of languages, however, are far fewer than outside the group, both in the nature of the language itself and in the information selected and available to the culture. The news and the world-view in Spain are still basically European. But just across the Strait of Gibraltar lie the Arab languages and the Arab world, where news is drawn not from nearby Spain but from Saudi Arabia and Iran, three thousand miles away.

And closer to home, we *choose* our consciousness at each moment—we are unaware of our bodies sitting in the chair as we read (note the weight of your body against the floor, your breathing), since we must further select our experience consciously in order to attain a stable consciousness. A proposed reconstruction in consciousness may seem beyond the pale to most of us, but then so would a description of the wonders of the telephone or the "miracle" of space flight seem otherworldly to the technically unsophisticated. If understood and trained, such a shift in consciousness might enable many to perform those "selfless" steps which could begin to more adequately act upon our contemporary collective problems.

The piecemeal and analytic mode of organizing thought and action, which has been long ingrained and has continually triumphed in the particular cultural evolution and material "ascent" of Western society, needs supplantation by a more complete, holistic perspective. Our cultural evolution has provided a secure material basis, but also the necessity for a development of a new conscious choice for ourselves, often referred to in the esoteric traditions of the East as "conscious evolution."

In contemporary life many people have sensed these necessities, often without knowing what they were sensing. Throughout our cultural history there have been many groups who have provided the means to develop this more complete human consciousness, yet the mainstream has never, at least in the West, really turned to them. These groups have always remained a very small minority, "esoteric" or deeply hidden, and their participation in the active development of science, art, and industry, as in the case of Newton, is rarely acknowledged. Since the mainstream in the West, especially in the past century, has turned further and further away from completeness, our current lack of a developed technology of consciousness has left a murky, stagnant area, which has spawned the charlatans, the fast-buck operators, the instant self-improvement teachers who come and go. Others have been led to a degenerated religious mysticism, which has been lifted *in toto* from another culture, the development of another time; to psychotherapies which promise much of an evolutionary nature but which only placate, stall, or backtrack; to instant Zen or pop yoga; to parapsychological "experiences" venerated as remote Africans venerated the flash of gunpowder; to searches for Shamans in the desert.

These early mistakes are to be found anywhere a new understanding is taking root. Much of the early excitement is generated by people who will not make much eventual use of that understanding. They may also proclaim this development as the ultimate panacea rather than merely constructive contribution. For most, the "search" has unfortunately become the mere substitution of one concept or idea for another. "Understanding one's feelings," "expanded orgasm" techniques, simpleminded meditation, "self-remembering," and awareness training follow one another around continually, among the same audience, year after year. Other people, attempting to restore an ancient tradition, restore only its superficial and superannuated aspects. I was recently invited to join a group whose devotion to ancient Tibet has led them to construct a replica of an ancient Tibetan monastery. These people, sincere as they are, do not seem to realize for whom these structures were originally intended, and into what cultural ground they are currently being set. I feel this is a useful example, since it merely makes external many of the patterns which I hope to define in this book. The search for an extended knowledge of oneself can lead to a "conscious evolution," a shift in our mode of understanding ourselves and our lives, complementary to our cultural and biological evolution. The need for this basic development currently fosters many diverse ideas and techniques, few of which, however, contain what their adherents seek.

"Look not at my outward shape but take what is in my hand."
—Rumi

3

A Cultural Hemianopia: Intuition and Brain Structure

There are moments, I suppose, that strike each of us as exceptionally significant, both in our personal and intellectual lives. One of mine was the day I started college. It was in New York City, in the late 1950s.

As background, I may add that my high-school education was especially useful to me. My first educational pursuit was physics. Physics seemed the most secure route to a hard knowledge of the nature of man and of the universe. But I found engineering and elementary physics and mathematics courses too lifeless to my taste, too divorced from people, from their thinking and feeling. The Romantic poets then captured my interest, but since I lacked elegance in my own writing and had a certain dissatisfaction with the limitless boundaries of pure prose, I turned to psychology, which I hoped would be a rigorous science, one which could consider the full complement of human phenomena. My understanding of philosophy and psychology was naïve, based on my own attempts at introspection, and on my study in high school of the works of Darwin and William James, wherein I was presented with the perspective of biological evolution, and of a psychology (at least in James's *Principles*) which did promise a completeness.

Given my interests, I signed up for five academic courses in my first college semester: English Literature of the Nineteenth Century, Calculus, Introduction to the Study of Psychology, Introduction to Philosophy, and a course titled (I think) "Freud and the Modern Mind." It is the last three which concern me here, and from which I have yet to fully recover.

I arrived at my psychology class with my impossibly idealistic freshman expectations: with the perspective of evolution integrated, after all, and with the scope provided by James, psychology had had seventy years or so to apply the various developments in hard science to a complete science of man.

When we were all seated, our professor arose. I recall (this was my very first college class) his appearance: a man in a gray-brown suit, quite overweight, with a large nose, and short sandy hair combed forward. My very first thought was that he looked like a giant rat. Professor X began, "I know that many of you are here because of an interest in your experience, a desire to find out what goes on in your thoughts, to understand abnormal consciousness and schizophrenia, and because of your interest in learning about ways in which your mind can operate.

"I want to tell you that psychology as you will learn it does not consider those questions as proper subjects for investigation. Psychology is, primarily, the study of scientific evidence, and of how a fact becomes worthy of science."

Save for the first part of his invocation, I would have been sure I had simply made a mistake: had I entered the wrong room perhaps (the school was new to me) or the wrong department? Perhaps I had entered Statistics 347B, or Introduction to Methodological Analysis 665F. For the remainder of the semester, we studied rats and taught them tricks which they did not want to learn and which we did not care to teach. And, gradually, my first impression of my professor deepened: academic psychology was a discipline fascinated with its technical achievement, which had lost much of its primary focus, and was content to treat Man as if he were a Giant Rat.

I had fewer expectations of philosophy, having read little on my own, and when a jocular young man presented his ideas, I was initially quite pleased. "Philosophy," he told us, "is what philosophers do," which seemed fine to me, and "The expression of an argument is always in inverse relationship to its presentation." He went on to discourse upon the idea of knowledge, and noted that "Knowledge is that which can be explicitly expressed in writing." Now this was, simply, amazing to me, and, as I watched everyone writing down these maxims (I never could master taking notes), I began to feel like poor Lemuel Gulliver among the philosophers.

The course on Freud did nothing to make me feel more at home. We were introduced to his exquisite genius for analyzing the symptoms of his patients, to his description of the "cures" for which he became famous, along with his equally monumental naïveté, the insularity in his attempts to characterize people of cultures and religious traditions foreign to him. I found here the same reductionism: the view that we are conscious of only what we can express in words. Freud's insight on the mechanisms of an "unconscious" led him too far: to group everything which we cannot express verbally into one dank, conceptual, hydraulic ooze to which were consigned willy-nilly religion, neurosis, repressed fears, and the esoteric practices of less technically developed cultures (of which Freud, by the way, knew little).

The conventional approach, in psychology, philosophy, and even in the most humanistic aspects of medicine, assumed that man could be studied from the outside, that knowledge and consciousness were completely reflected in words or actions. In logico-philosophic analysis, objective psychology, and psychoanalysis, the remainder of our nature is an "unconscious" inhabited only by the blind emotion or neurotic religion of the Freudians, "the future of an illusion," nonsensical questions rejected by the Logical Positivists, and old-fashioned pseudo-problems disdained by the Behaviorists. Two years later I was on leave, on a freight ship bound west, from New York to New York, and reading alternative approaches to consciousness and knowledge between stopovers in Africa and in the Far and Middle East. A complementary approach seemed more attainable.

When one speaks, as I did in the previous chapter, of the possibility of a change in consciousness, a change in which relationships that are normally obscure become clear, many people can only imagine a ghostlike connection between objects, a gossamer entity connected to "another world." These distortions of our imagination are, in part, due to a degeneration of the metaphors of esoteric and religious tradition and to a consideration of hypothetical schema as if they were real, rather than conceptual, entities. Thus, for centuries people have laboriously attempted to turn lead into gold, to "awaken" a physical "third eye," to physically enter "another world." In the last case we see a possible genesis of belief in unidentified flying objects, in many "higher consciousness" groupings. Yet "another world" should be understood as metaphor, sometimes overextended as in our culture. Properly, the metaphor of "another world" is usually intended to signify such as "the world of dreams," or even "the financial world," which is equally mysterious to many non-initiates.

According to esoteric tradition, the "organ of perception," which can be tutored in the same fashion as is language, is what we term intuition. Although the phrase is often maligned, conventionally used to indicate random guesswork or a mysterious combination of elements, it should be properly understood as *knowledge without recourse to inference.* The diverse and seemingly unconnected practices of religious and esoteric traditions center around the cultivation of what we might call nonlinear immediate understanding, in complement to the inferential, meditated, ordered sequence of "rational" thought. The metaphor of sight is often employed; it is like explaining to a blind man what color is like. If a man has cataracts, for instance, and thus an unrealized potential for sight, we should take him to an eye surgeon who can aid in the removal of his occlusions, rather than engage in innumerable discussions of what he is missing. This is why most members of a true esoteric tradition are less interested in Armchair Metaphysics than is normally assumed.

The many discussions which stem from an outmoded cosmology (such as a Ptolemaic universe *), and ideas about a "ray" of creation, flying saucers, and so forth, are not very useful. A teacher of esoteric tradition, Salih of Merv, was asked, "Illuminate your abstruse subject for me"; he replied, "The blind need eyes, not light."

The techniques of religious and esoteric traditions are "illogical" by intent. They employ music, dance, movement, specific body postures, creative spatial visualization· and techniques designed to defeat ordinary linear, sequential thinking, such as concentrative meditation, Zen koans, and the literature of the Sufi tradition. A Sufi was taken on a tour of a rich braggart's building, shown room after room of priceless artifacts, and was asked, "What impressed you most of all?" He replied, "The fact that the earth is strong enough to support the weight of such a massive building."

Those of esoteric tradition insist that their activities are "not for your mind," which means not for the verbal, inferential apparatus of the mind. When we speak of a person possessing a "great mind" we often mean no more than that he or she has a great mouth, a way with words. Logical, scientific, and verbal presentations are honored in our society. Less honored are spatial ability, grace in movement, and those aspects of a comprehensive awareness of relationships between objects or ideas which do not translate well into words.

Following Freud, and other cultural prejudices, we conventionally oppose the faculty of reason with *passion*, a blind, freewheeling, and diffuse activation, a conception which links rage, emotionality, and religion quite indiscriminately. We share

---

* It should be noted that the "flat earth" theory, the "geocentric" universe, and others such as the "Elements" of Greek tradition were originally metaphors and myths regarding the mind. It is only metaphysical inflation that has caused these to degenerate into confused descriptions of the earth and universe. They appear silly and primitive today as scientific descriptions, yet this was not their intent. And some today still seek "cosmic principles," or a sense of the universe.

a common anxiety that everything outside the province of rational thought is *irrational,* and is to be feared and avoided. This statement is quite accurate linguistically, yet may be misleading in its implications. Properly opposed to the verbal-analytic process of reason should not be passion but intuition. The logical mode of knowledge operates sequentially, arriving at a truth inferentially, proceeding logically from one element to another. Intuition operates simultaneously, is concerned with the sets of relations among elements, which receive their meaning from the overall holistic context.

Reason, then, primarily involves an analysis of discrete elements, inferentially (sequentially) linked; intuition involves a simultaneous perception of the whole. The word "rational" is derived from "ration," to break into segments. The common element in actions normally considered "intuitive"—a great insight, a superb dance movement, an immediate reaction in sports, an overall picture of a finished object or building design —is a simultaneity of perception.

It is not the individual, discrete objects, elements, or even ideas which are themselves changed in the shift from a logical mode of consciousness to an intuitive one. Rather, it is the relationship between the elements which change, and the interpretation of a given bit of sensory data may be different depending upon context. The famous blind man may indeed decide that he is touching three separate unrelated objects in sequence, which he might guess are a rug, a column, and a vacuum cleaner, when he is touching an elephant three times. If his sight could be restored he would note that his piecemeal approach had led him astray; that he misinterpreted the available sensory information for lack of an intuitive, overall appreciation of the whole. The deficiency that those of us who are not physically blind share is that we overvalue the verbal mode; we believe what we are told (especially if it is written), and this can unduly increase the control of rational, analytic verbal processes in our lives.

Mulla Nasrudin wished to get rid of several annoying boys and constructed a false and intriguing story about a feast which was supposedly being offered. As he elaborated his story further and further, the boys ran off to the feast. Nasrudin followed them, saying, "It *might* be true after all," after considering his own persuasive story.

If Western science is predominantly based upon sequential and analytic procedures for analysis, explication, and verification, then why not consider the possibility that several of the supposedly "incomprehensible" disciplines and theories of the East are based upon a complementary mode of consciousness? In *Theoretical Foundations of Chinese Medicine*, the German Sinologist Manfred Porkert thus contrasts the foci of Chinese and Western sciences:

> Chinese medicine, like the other Chinese sciences, defines data on the basis of the inductive and synthetic mode of cognition. Inductivity corresponds to a logical link between two effective positions existing at the same time in different places in space. (Conversely, causality is the logical link between two effective positions given at different times at the same place in space.) In other words, effects based on positions that are separate in space yet simultaneous in time are mutually inductive and thus are called *inductive effects*. In Western science prior to the development of electrodynamics and nuclear physics (which are founded essentially on inductivity), the inductive nexus was limited to subordinate uses in protosciences such as astrology. Now Western man, as a consequence of two thousand years of intellectual tradition, persists in the habit of making causal connections first and, inductive links, if at all, only as an afterthought. This habit must still be considered the biggest obstacle to an adequate appreciation of Chinese science in general and of Chinese medicine in particular.

In a separate paper Dr. Porkert notes the complementary aspects of reality delineated by the two modes:

The scientist seeking insights by way of the inductive and synthetic mode of cognizance will observe first and afterwards speculate on his observations; the scientist applying the causal and analytic mode in his quest for knowledge will speculate and act first and observe afterwards. In other words, by being receptive at the first step and active at the second step, the actual, momentary functions, the dynamic aspect of reality will be perceived and defined. By keying the active (speculative or physical) intervention to the first step—thus mentally or even physically obliterating the network of dynamic functions—and the receptive attitude to the second step, the substratums supporting the functions, the static aspect of reality will be perceived and defined.

In China, as well as in other countries, many diverse practices are employed in the development of a dynamic, simultaneous mode of consciousness. The exercises of Tai Chi Ch'uan, Kung Fu, and the martial arts are rudimentary training systems of simultaneous actuation. The use of movement, dance, and other bodily activities has led to an interest in sports as a Western variant of these practices. We note, for instance, that classical Greek education (albeit only for a small, elite band of men) emphasized the complementarity of physical and intellectual development. In classical Islam, too, there was little or no conflict between "two cultures"; an education for both modes of knowledge was emphasized.

In response to a growing awareness that our education lacks completeness, and as another example of the Western reductionist mentality, "Mystical Sport Centers" have been set up for those on the encounter, massage, self-preoccupation circuit. Ordinary sports are proclaimed as a "Western yoga." The difficulty here is the same as with the elephant in the dark: these proponents of "sport as mysticism" mistake one external aspect of a comprehensive education for the whole, and do not sense the relationship of their activities to what they intend. Sports, which might aid in the initial rudimentary development of a fluid simultaneity of mind, is claimed as the goal, the jock-strap as the icon.

In the esoteric and religious tradition of the Middle and Far East, these various, isolated, movement and sport activities are intended to acquaint people with the basics of a mode of consciousness that might later be developed into a "deeper understanding," a more holistic comprehension. In this fashion do the dances, exercises, and postures of esoteric tradition aid in the construction of a capability of simultaneous perception. If properly transferred at a later time into the "metaphysical" realm, this physical ability enables a more comprehensive perception, a "wisdom." It is, however, more easily done than said.

A proper analogy to this form of esoteric education is the learning of language. In each type of education, an invisible "organ" of mental function is developed. We often do not credit that it is only in the past century that we have seen a large-scale development of the "organ" of language in the West, with the rise of compulsory schooling and consequent high literacy.

Language depends predominantly upon sequence: letters follow a certain order to comprise words, words in a certain order (or within certain prescribed sets of orders) fashion sentences, sentences must sequentially develop thoughts to convey meaning. If we scramble sentences, our meaning is lost. If we alter spelling, we are no longer conveying language. The law, a most logically structured system, depends predominantly upon precedent and sequence, and upon language. It is, along with science and formal logic, one of the most refined developments of the analytic mode, and it is a cornerstone of our contemporary social order. Yet, if we were to try to educate a person from a group of illiterates to practice law, we should have to begin with instruction in the letters of the alphabet, and in the specifics of their possible combinations. He might become excited, for instance, at having learned the difference between *act* and *cat*, and, since that would be a new development for him and perhaps for his community of illiterates, he might immediately leave to set up

a "growth center" to enlighten others. In a contemporary population of spiritual illiterates, it is no wonder that we witness similar
actions.

Music, crafts, dances, visualizations, postures, martial arts,
sport—they do not depend *predominantly* upon sequence, although sequence is certainly involved. They each convey the basis of a simultaneous mode of intuitive thought, yet are not
necessarily goals themselves. The higher levels of intuition, of
wisdom, of "deep understanding" in esoteric tradition, bear the
same relationship to the "sport as yoga" movement (or to
much else of what is common today on the American spiritual
frontier) as trial law does to spelling.

I propose, then, two complementary principles in human
mentation: an ordered sequencer which underlies language and
"rational" mentation, and a simultaneous processor employed
for coordination of movement in space, for artistic creativity
and reception, for the tonal aspect of music, and for other
functions which I subsume under intuition, a faculty of holistic
perception. The perception of the holistic aspects of reality demands, as Manfred Porkert points out, a simultaneous mode of
experience. Both the sequential and the simultaneous modes
have their proper levels of functioning and interaction. Most of
us have been educated and have developed sequential abilities
(readin', 'ritin' and 'rithmetic) at the expense of the fluid and
simultaneous. Many, well-trained verbally, say they cannot "understand" art; the rationalist opposes the "mystic," partly because we attribute only our verbal-analytic abilities to our
"mind" while often denying "mental" status to the intuitive. We
may compliment a painter or photographer's "eye," a crafts-
man's "touch," an artist for an apt "gut" feeling—and rarely
for the powers of their mind.

This second, holistic, area of human specialization has, as
far as the mainstream is concerned, been left fallow in the
West since the Renaissance, with the divorce of science from an
admittedly degenerated religion. We do not educate intuition

since it seems to us to lack a basis, and it is often confused with the negative connotation of the "irrational"—or with sloppy thinking, with an ineffable "women's sense" when women are being devalued, with the apparently failed thinkers of Eastern societies that have lacked our materialist progress.

It is time to give the simultaneous aspect of our consciousness its due place in our understanding of the mind, in our education, and in human affairs. Intuition is not an obscure, mysterious function possessed by only a very few highly creative and unusual artists or scientists who produce interesting theories. Intuition is a faculty considered largely negative—creativity is romanticized, made external, considered unavailable to most ordinary people. The faculty of intuition is, rather, latent in all of us, a primary aspect of our cognitive abilities which we have allowed to degenerate.

The esoteric metaphor of our "blindness" is quite apt, and can be extended. "Hemianopia" is a blindness to half the visual world, due to lesions in one half of the brain. Damage to or lack of proper development in the occiput (visual area) of half of the brain can often leave a person unaware of half of his visual world, although the eye and the visual system may remain intact. (Of course, damage to both sides will render the individual completely blind.) Our contemporary education yields a similar disorder: we may have developed one half of our ability to organize external reality to an unparalleled extent, yet remain "blind," or at least hemianopic, to the other. Mainstream education is specialized to develop only half of the mind.

Albert Einstein, in describing his own special scientific abilities, remarked, "The really valuable thing is intuition." He described his thought processes as "combinatory play." "Combinatory play" does indeed describe half of the brain's operation. The antagonism between the modes of intuition and analysis, and our associations of these two modes with the sides of the body, stem from the duality and separation of function of the brain. We speak of "dexterity," of a feeling of "rightness," of the law in French as *le droit;* and, on the other hand, we define negative things as "sinister," "gauche," "maladroit." The brain's control of the body is actually "crossed," with the left cerebral hemisphere controlling the right side of the body and the right side of visual and auditory space; the right hemisphere's responsibilities are to the left. For over a century it has been known that language depends predominantly (in right-handed people) on the functioning of the left hemisphere of the cerebral cortex, and more recently it has been discovered that spatial abilities depend upon the right. Evidence of this is based upon studies which show that lesions of the left hemisphere in right-handed people interfere with language, while lesions restricted to the right hemisphere usually do not. Left-handers are a more complex group. In some of them, brain organization is identical to right-handers', in some it is reversed, and some show a "mixed dominance"—language ability on both sides. This third group, which may include some people suffering from birth complications, may be responsible for increases in stuttering and dyslexia in left-handers and for reports of decreased spatial ability. This group of left-handers may have difficulty because the sequential information-processing which underlies language may interfere with the simultaneous activity necessary for spatial abilities. And perhaps a reason why the two modes of information-processing are maintained by two separated segmental hemispheres is to reduce the potential interference of one mode on the other. It is difficult to describe verbally how to ride a bicycle, which requires a simultaneous "touch." Similarly, too much simultaneous verbal information-processing may upset a lineal argument, or a sentence structure.

The functions of the hemispheres, then, are not *entirely* binary with all language in the left and all spatial abilities in the right. For instance, almost all forms of language contain some simultaneous components, as in much creative prose and poetry, and there are many sequential elements involved in spatial endeavors. The left hemisphere may bear *primary* responsibility for language, but it does not bear all the burden. If it is severely damaged, the remaining ability may be below a threshold for effective function. More correctly, we can consider any one situation a unique blend of sequence and simultaneity, and can consider whether the brain operates differentially in these tasks. Language input in the brain may largely involve sequence, as in reading or listening, but once data have entered, both the sequential and simultaneous elements can operate. Information can enter primarily through one hemisphere, and then be sent to the other for further processing and output through either side. In addition to this cooperation, each hemisphere seems to develop some additional emergency "backup" capability for the other, with, presumably, some minor sequential abilities in the right, simultaneous ones in the left. The hemispheres are specialized, then, for different modes of consciousness and thought, not primarily for different types of situations. The right hemisphere participates to some minor extent in speech, the left in spatial abilities.

In the analysis of the function of the living brain, it is quite important to study not only the *potential* for the hemispheres' involvement in any situation, but their *actual* involvement. Employing data from brain damage and neurosurgical cases, many investigators have charted the potential capabilities of differing areas of the two hemispheres. These neurosurgical data are sometimes not relevant to the general case since they are based on disorders unique in their complexity and which in an injured person are often combined with other diseases or injuries. Such lesion or disconnection studies might, for instance, show that the right hemisphere possesses the basic capability for several rudimentary language functions. In normal use, however, the specific right-hemisphere processes might rarely be employed, since the left hemisphere is generally more proficient. There is, furthermore, a difficulty in immediate generalization from biological potential to actual function. A biological advantage need not be binary for it to predominate physiologically. If two identical bakeries, with equal capacities and similar products, were competing in a neighborhood, and one charged 5 percent less for bread, it would receive a disproportionately large share of the business.

In our laboratory investigations at the Langley-Porter Neuropsychiatric Institute we have made a special point of studying normal, uninjured people, who are performing everyday tasks, and we have developed a method to determine which hemisphere is more active at any moment within a given situation. David Galin, our colleagues, and I have found, using a surface electroencephalograph (EEG) which passively records brain activity, that in most "rational" tasks, such as language processing, the left hemisphere (in right-handed people) is more active than is the right, and that in intuitive tasks the right hemisphere is more active than the left. Our own studies, buttressed by increasing evidence of differences in people's reaction time to verbal and to spatial stimuli, eye movement changes,* and dichotic listening experiments, confirm that normal people do make use of the potential differential specializations of the two cerebral hemispheres.

This finding is not a phenomenon based on a few neurosurgical cases, but on studies of thousands of ostensibly normal people. The fact that so many people in everyday situations do employ their brain bifunctionally provides neurophysiological support for the existence of the two divergent modes of consciousness; for the concrete possibility of educating both halves of the brain; and for a rapprochement between exclusively "intellectual" and "intuitive" approaches to knowledge.

It is also important to note, in the context of the traditional esoteric psychologies, that the recent discovery of a right-hemisphere activation in intuitive cognition does not *reduce* the mental aspects of esoteric knowledge to "right-brain functioning." It does not allow a person who might be interested in a

---

* If you ask someone to spell "Mississippi," he will make more eye movements to the right than if you ask him to imagine the river itself.

more complete consciousness to decide merely that he or she "understands" it as an "activity for the right hemisphere." The comparison again is with learning language: one might realize that language depends predominantly upon the left hemisphere, but this useful realization does not constitute *learning language*. One must still study grammar, spelling, writing, etc.

The studies of the role of the right hemisphere in cognition do, however, provide a secure physiological basis for areas of thought often devalued in contemporary Western society. When different remedies for the same illness, which are employed in numerous and isolated societies, are found to have a common physiological basis, we can understand the unity within the apparent diversity. We can then choose the method of preparation best suited to our needs. We do not now understand esoteric tradition enough to judge the efficacy of certain processes, but we are beginning to understand the common mode of esoteric activity, especially the diverse methods and techniques used to train intuition. Thus, the practices of meditation, of whirling, chanting, the ritual movements of Tai Chi Ch'uan, the martial arts, the design of the Gothic cathedrals and the temples of Islam intended to have an immediate effect on a person, complex geometric symbols, Arabic geometrical design, the postures of Hatha Yoga and other exercises share a common physiological basis. Their "site of action" is the simultaneous information-processing of the right hemisphere of the human brain, an "organ of perception" present, but undeveloped, in everyone.

We now possess both a new understanding of ancient systems of knowledge and a technical basis for the analysis of the human brain. It is now the time to undo the cultural bias against intuition as a mode of knowledge, against, effectively, the right hemisphere. Our culture and education often produce people hemianopic to reality, and it is time to return toward wholeness—not merely through a faddish concentration on individual processes of the esoteric tradition, but through an attention to goals.

4

On Psychiatroid
Mentation
and the
Esoteric Traditions

Six blind medical students sat by the gate of a great city as an elephant was led slowly past. Inspired by scientific curiosity of the highest degree, the six blind students rushed forward to palpate the great beast and to determine the nature of his being.

The first man's hands fell upon the elephant's tusks. "Ah," said he, "this creature is a thing of bones; they even protrude through his skin." Later on, years having past, this man became an orthopedist.

At the same time the second blind medical student seized the elephant's trunk and identified its function. "What a nose!" he exclaimed. "Surely this is the most important part of the animal." Accordingly he became a rhinologist.

The third man chanced upon the elephant's great flapping ear and came to a similar conclusion; for him the ear was everything, so he, in time, became an otologist.

The fourth rested his hands on the huge chest and abdomen of the elephant. "The contents of this barrel must be enormous," he thought, "and the pathological derangements infinite in number and variety." Nothing would do but that he should become an internist.

One of the blind men caught hold of the elephant's tail. "This," he said, "would appear to be a useless appendage. It might even be a source of trouble. Better take it off." The blind man became a surgeon.

But the last of the six men did not depend upon the sense of touch. Instead he only listened. He had heard the elephant approaching, the rattle of chains and the shouts of the keepers.

It may be that he heard the elephant heaving a great sigh as he trudged along. "Where is the creature going?" he asked. No one answered. "Where did he come from?" he asked. No one knew.

Then this man fell into a deep reverie. What was in the elephant's mind, he wondered, in having left wherever he was and having come to this great city? Why does he submit to the indignities of our curiosity and the slavery of chains? And while he was wondering how to find out the answers to these questions the elephant was gone.

This man became a psychiatrist.

The other students were disgusted at this impracticality. They turned their backs upon their visionary companion. What difference does it make, said they, what the elephant's purposes may be? And his chains—they constitute a legal not a medical problem. The important thing is to recognize the animal's structure!

Then they fell to quarreling among themselves as to whether the elephant's structure was primarily that of a nose or that of an ear or that of a tail. And although they all differed flatly from one another on these points they all agreed that the psychiatrist was a fool.

—Adapted slightly from Karl Menninger's story
"The Cinderella of Medicine"

I

Because we do not conventionally educate, perceive, or credit a holistic, intuitive mode of knowledge, we find that reductions, substitutes, and palliatives are elevated beyond their nominal functions. This, in some part, has contributed to the unwarranted extension of psychiatry and psychoanalysis from a doctrinal, experimental approach to a quite specific and limited set of mental dysfunctions in early-twentieth-century Vienna to an overall cultural theory—an extension that exemplifies what should be termed "psychiatroid mentation." The doctrines of psychoanalysis may, for instance, have been initially useful in elucidating the possible sexual etiology of certain personal problems, but they have become fragmented and culture-bound in the attempt to generalize from this minor achievement to a general theory of human nature and human possibility.

Like the reductionism inherent in behaviorism, we find many of the most important human needs and developments reduced, not to muscle twitches or observable action, but to the hydrodynamics of sexual fluid. This was not an early, elementary error corrected in the development of psychoanalysis, for at the end of his career, in *Moses and Monotheism*, Sigmund Freud reiterated the statement "religious experience can be accounted for by the same means as neurotic processes."

This is the sort of elementary mistake which takes root largely because of our cultural hemianopia, our inability to organize the simultaneous aspects of reality and to perceive the functions of religious and esoteric traditions. One reason not to base our understanding of man on psychotherapy, whether of psychoanalytic or other persuasion, is that psychotherapy has permeated our culture largely unchecked by the normal processes of scientific evaluation.

Consider the question of the efficacy of psychotherapeutic treatment, since it should provide a secure empirical basis for many conceptual schema which have passed into daily discourse as if they were proven fact, such as "ego," "libido," and personality "complexes." If psychotherapy is not an empirical science, then its claims as a key to human nature should be discounted, along with the claims of other transient pop anthropologies, psychologies, sociologies, and "awareness trainings." The question to consider is whether, if psychotherapy produces its claimed results, the gains of treatment outweigh the risk. Based on the reams of evidence that have been presented in research journals so far, I do not think, for example, the practice of psychotherapy would be offered on a paid, continuing basis to the public if it had to pass the conventional requirements the Food and Drug Administration imposes for a new medicine.

Studies of psychotherapy initiated by Hans Eysenck in England after the Second World War often show that people who undergo psychotherapy, especially psychoanalysis, if they are chosen at random from many seeking it, do not benefit more than those who are denied it. Several more recent studies indicate that some forms of psychotherapy make some people better, others worse, with only a shade more showing improvement rather than decline. This evidence of a lack of empirical success on the part of psychoanalysis often comes as a surprise to the public at large, and to those culturally influenced by psychiatroid mentation, since "cures" are much discussed and dramatized, failures less so.

A recent research report of the Menninger Foundation focuses primarily on which therapies can be effective for different people and different problems. This is by far the most useful research approach, since it may lead away from the general "bloodletting" procedures which characterized the early psychoanalytic therapies. With an understanding of the dominant role of the therapist's personality, we may be able to develop a more balanced spectrum of treatments for different difficulties and different people. Yet the research evidence up to now should not give weight to a psychiatroid claim to any special insight into the nature of man. On the other hand, many other research studies by staunch defenders of the discipline claim a great spread in the subsequent effects of psychotherapy compared with control subjects (more improve, more get worse). On the basis of such data we are often invited to consider therapy effective. However, these findings support only an argument for the *existence of a phenomenon*, such as might be appropriate in the case of ESP, not support for a specific medical treatment or for a consistent view of man. We would not validate a surgical theory if the results showed only that a few patients improve following surgery and a few become worse. Psychotherapy, as a practice and as a body of knowledge, must be considered to be in an infant stage of development, a stage in which responsible investigators are attempting to discover and to develop a proper discipline of treatment. It should certainly not be considered a mature science or as proven knowledge about the nature of man. It is not even clear that, in view of the data on the effects of the treatment, psychotherapy should be offered to the general public on anything but a tentative and experimental basis.

Consider the training and the qualifications of psychotherapists to cross disciplines which touch on human nature. Ernest Poser, of McGill University in Montreal, found in treating schizophrenic patients that randomly selected undergraduates produced more positive change than did psychiatrists and psychiatric social workers. We would be very much surprised if such a difference occurred, for instance, between those trained and untrained in neurosurgery. Dr. Poser's and others' studies indicate that the "training" of psychotherapists is less relevant than one would ordinarily assume.

This is not to say that there exist no successful psychotherapeutic interactions, no generally effective psychotherapists, but rather that the doctrinal and intellectual training in schools of therapies is not terribly helpful. The actual practice of psychotherapy and of psychotherapeutic treatments are much more alike across varying doctrines than the doctrines themselves would imply. And, as Jerome Frank's analysis in *Persuasion and Healing* makes clear, similarities exist in widely divergent cultures as well: the faith healer, witch doctor, the shaman or medicine man; patients enter psychotherapy demoralized, and are given hope by the process. Unfortunately, the specific focus, doctrines, and rituals of several psychotherapies have become the Totems of our society, *our* society's contemporary version of astrology or oracular consultation. This is not to malign psychiatric treatment, since it often seems to "work." Perhaps, however, its success is due more to the personal characteristics of the practitioners than to the theoretic structure.

Carl Rogers, a most influential American psychotherapist and one most willing to initiate careful study, has found that the specific qualities that make for successful therapy involve the personality of the therapist, not the efficacy of theory or dogma. These personal characteristics include empathy, spontaneity, and the therapist's "unconditional positive regard" for the client. Rogers concludes that "Intellectual training [for psychotherapists] and the acquiring of information has, I believe, many valuable results—but becoming a therapist is not one of those results." Psychotherapeutic training may, by the very nature of its irrelevance to the situation (especially in academic medicine), exclude many who might be its best practitioners (Rogers' "empathetic" people), much as the selection process often works in contemporary political life.

The practitioners of a therapy, whether psychoanalytic, nondirective, "humanistic," implosive, "rational-emotive," or even shamanistic, may falsely read their "successes" as a strengthening of their own theoretical approach (even when their successes may not greatly outweigh their failures), and then attempt to apply this doctrine to religion, art, or anthropology. This has occurred often, notably in the case of psychoanalysis. If we step back from the current craze for therapy in all forms, and the psychiatroid mentation engendered by literary means such as the psychoanalysis of "primitive" cultures, or the plays of Eugene O'Neill which are suffused by the doctrine, we find here the cult system of our own time, and unverified, rootless belief in an unsupported doctrine. Its overgeneralization is best symbolized by a blind person who may have gotten hold of the mysterious elephant, but only by the balls.

II

Then what of the relationship between psychotherapy and the esoteric traditions? Perhaps the greatest difficulty is that the talking psychotherapies have, for many people, usurped the status of a training of their intuition and substituted the doctrine's preoccupations for the individual's own. All human endeavors relate to an understanding of the meaning of life, and psychiatry can claim no precedence over, say, mechanical engineering, particle physics, or shoe repair. Yet there is some confusion regarding their proper role among the psychotherapists themselves, and they are often placed in an inappropriate position by their clients.

In the absence of a mainstream spiritual tradition competent in its area of specialization, people have turned to those who offer them the promise and the hope of integration, development, calmness, relaxation, and comprehensive understanding. I believe that we have lost sight of the fact that psychotherapists are trained almost exclusively in dealing with human dysfunction; and (as we considered above) if that training is perhaps not appropriate even for its intended use, it certainly would not automatically yield license to practice in other areas. There is no training generally offered to psychotherapists in the technology of developing and understanding extended modes of consciousness. Often mental "dysfunctions" or difficulties are merely lumped together by psychotherapists with any genuine "unusual experiences" or evidence of extended consciousness. Psychotherapists have little formal training in discriminating these dimensions of consciousness, and often reduce their clients' experience to conform to their own doctrine.

Difficulties are also inherent in the normal practice and clientele of therapists. A psychotherapist who might work exclusively in consultation with physicians, lawyers, or social or rehabilitation workers may find himself the "local expert" on all things mental. Since in our society there is often no one of greater, trained competence in mental phenomena to consult, the psychotherapist may come to assume that his area of expertise is greater than that for which he was trained, even though his training was only the study of mental dysfunction (and, in the case of a psychiatrist, medicine).

I travel and lecture, and often I am asked by psychiatrists and psychotherapists what they should do about patients who inquire about meditation, or their unusual personal experiences, or their glimpses of an extended perception. "Am I crazy?" these patients ask. I usually inquire of the therapists whether they have been trained to be specialists in these areas, and whether their training has specifically encompassed these dimensions of conscious experience, or whether their training was restricted to alcoholism, suicide, sexual or marriage problems, anxiety attacks, uncontrollable violence, and the like. If a psychiatrist, for example, has had no training in this traditional human specialization, then he or she should either obtain such training (which is unfortunately quite difficult) or at the very least cease citing and applying a supposed theoretical and professional authority where there exists no such special authority. It could be argued that psychotherapists are at a particular disadvantage here since they often attempt to apply mistaken and reductionistic concepts from irrelevant areas of their training (as in the case of "psychohistory"), instead of realizing that their own training and expertise are inappropriate.

Psychiatroid mentation reduces the dimensions of human consciousness to those which we can verbally and rationally express, in the same manner as has much of contemporary psychology and philosophy. This type of thought has unfortunately caused an unwarranted extension of unverified theoretical schema into everyday life, such as the "unconscious," "Oedipus complexes," "reaction formations," "religion as an illusion."

Freud set out a hydraulic model of personality, explained in the context of the operations of simple nineteenth-century machinery and of early developments in physiology. This model postulates a mental "energy" which shifts from a consciousness exclusively verbal and rational to an uncharted, feared "unconscious" that contains "repressed" hatred, ancient memories, unsocial lusts, and religious experience. It is an outmoded, ethnocentric conceptual model of the mind that has been embraced by the culture despite its lack of correctness.

Traditional psychotherapy has often reduced a concern with

conscious evolution, or religious interest, to the level of personal neurosis, often to sexual longings. The reverse may, however, be just as likely, since many human satisfactions can substitute for one another. In a culture such as ours, which often ignores possibilities for "conscious evolution," people may turn to secondary concerns, such as continual sexual, emotional, or social gratification, and even psychotherapy. The idea that all religion, all spirituality, all interest in esoteric tradition is always neurotic is clearly a function of our cultural hemianopia. The fallacious dichotomy between the high "conscious" level of reason and the lower depths of "passion" or of the "unconscious" has influenced many and has produced an unjustified, Victorian, and xenophobic fear of the esoteric tradition.*

The intent of religious and esoteric systems has always been to convey an intuitive wisdom of the purpose of life—certainly an intention which is not fairly described as neurotic. Many psychotherapists may become interested in a more comprehensive consciousness, but their overtraining in some areas and lack of it in others assure that they often cannot separate even their own desire for wisdom from their personal, transient difficulties. This difficulty is partly, I think, an occupational hazard of psychotherapy. After listening to and considering only personal problems day after day, the practitioner may become accustomed to viewing the world as a set of continual, identifiable problems. He or she may lose sight of other possibilities. Rumi: "If you spend time gazing at the floor, you will never see the ceiling."

This extreme psychiatroid concentration upon neurotic pathology causes people to look to other areas for help. Today, in our culture, the narrowness of the Freudian views sends unsatisfied seekers careening wildly in other directions: they may seek a solu-

---

* The comedian Woody Allen recently said of psychoanalysis: "When I first started going I feared that my personality would be changed to conform to a typical middle-class Viennese of the twenties. Now, I'd be willing to settle for that."

tion to their personal problems through a misguided involvement in aspects of esoteric tradition. Our lack of appreciation of these traditions causes some to reduce them, others to inflate their own personal problems to the metaphysical level. Individuals and, worse, psychotherapists "into" mysticism mistakenly mix disciplines, and confuse the contexts of various exercises and techniques. They may include in their offerings concepts from psychoanalysis, "sensitivity training," morning meditations, personality schema which give a satisfying name (or, better, number) to difficulties, work on the "chakras," unusual diets and exercises, and many other techniques. The best possible result of such an approach is that people get their fill of techniques, and learn lots of names and outmoded ideas. Most people, however, simply waste their time, and are either completely turned off to the ideas of the esoteric traditions or become blindly accepting of whatever is fed them. The esoteric traditions are not psychotherapies, and they cannot be understood in the same terms.

The psychiatroid orientation can lead people to regard the teachers and students of an esoteric discipline as if they were working on a reduced neurotic level. Such distortions result from an inefficient and mistaken deployment of personal characteristics of the teachers, rather than the substance of the teaching, much as a person who hates his high-school trigonometry instructor may develop a hatred for all mathematics. In a recent interview, Idries Shah commented that when some people who visit him do not get an immediate and obviously expanded consciousness, they instead take away small objects from around his house, such as ashtrays, books, etc. In our culture, we are offered little training in separating a personality from his ideas, the essence from the package. In my experience, these reductionist tendencies are inherent in psychiatroid mentation. There is a saying in India: "When a pickpocket looks at a saint, he sees only his pockets."

III

Unfortunately, many people influenced by psychiatroid thought confuse the search for an extended perspective on one's life with a new form of self-indulgence. It is often observed that people involved in psychotherapy become changed. What they really become is suddenly fascinated with their own personal problems. They may often discuss *ad nauseum* their emotional, sexual, and intellectual difficulties, until there is little else about which they are concerned, exemplifying Rumi's maxim.

Not by coincidence, these tendencies are all too common among the "personal growth" adherents as well. The same self-preoccupation is here confused with "growth," now merely re-directed from the observation of depression to the quest for ecstasy or emotion. "Why, I had the most terrific experience of *energy* in my Bioenergetics/Gestalt/Massage session last night," or "Sorry I can't help you, I'm really into experiencing my anger these days." These may be the manifestations of a new discipline: *Tantrum Yoga,* one might call it, the yoga of infantil-ism and self-preoccupation.

Self-indulgence is also often confused with following an esoteric discipline, as when a person adopts a particular tech-nique, such as self-observation, but uses it in a fragmentary, partial manner. What this approach does not credit is that if one is concentrating merely on oneself, it matters little whether one finds the self fascinating, disgusting, or even "objective." The point is that *all attention is directed at the self,* and nothing is left for a more comprehensive awareness. This kind of thinking stems from a simple confusion: self-indulgence is not mysticism. It is as mistaken as if a cell in the body decided that, by simple, continuous observation of its vicissitudes, it could somehow be-come a whole person. As I pointed out in the first chapter, in any real attempt at conscious development, attention needs to be di-rected *away* from the self, from the psychotherapeutic "growth"

or emotional levels, and away from piecemeal mystical techniques as well, in order that a person may encounter aspects of
his surroundings *other* than the ordinary self. In an undegener-
ated esoteric tradition, the ordinary self is not to be continually
massaged, pandered to, affirmed, or even "observed," but merely
set aside as an unreliable judge of events outside its province.
Here is a story from Idries Shah's *The Magic Monastery:*

A certain Sufi master was walking along a country road with
one of his disciples. The disciple said:
"I know that the best day of my life was when I decided
to seek you out, and when I discovered that through your
Presence I would find myself."
The Sufi said:
"Decision, whether for support or opposition, is a thing
which you do not know until you know it. You do not know
it through thinking that you know it."
The disciple said:
"Your meaning is obscure to me, and your statement is
dark and your intention is veiled from me."
The master said:
"You will in a few moments see something about the value
of decision, and who it is that makes decisions."
Presently they came to a meadow, where a farm worker
was throwing a stick to a dog. The Sufi said:
"I will count five, and he will throw three sticks to the
dog."
Sure enough, when the Sufi had so counted, the man
picked up three sticks and threw them to the dog, even
though they were out of earshot and the man had not seen
the pair.
Now the Sufi said:
"I will count three, and the man will sit down."
As soon as he had counted to three, the man did indeed
sit down, suddenly, on the ground.
Now the disciple, full of wonder, said:

"Could he be induced to raise his arms into the air?"

The Sufi nodded and, as they watched, the man's hands rose towards the sky.

The disciple was amazed, but the Sufi said:

"Let us now approach this man and speak with him."

When they had saluted the farm worker, the Sufi said to him:

"Why did you throw three sticks instead of one for the dog to retrieve?"

The farm man answered:

"I decided to do it as a test, to see whether he could follow more than one stick."

"So it was your own decision?"

"Yes," said the man, "nobody told me to do it."

"And," said the Sufi, "why did you sit down so suddenly?"

"Because I thought I would rest."

"Did anyone suggest it?"

"There is nobody here to suggest it."

"And when you raised your arms in the air, why was that?"

"Because I decided that it was lazy to sit on the ground, and I felt that raising my arms towards the Heavens would indicate that I should work rather than rest, and that inspiration to overcome laziness came from on high."

"Was that a decision of your own and nobody else's?"

"There was, indeed, nobody to make such a decision for me, and in any case it followed from my previous action."

The Sufi now turned to the disciple and said:

"Immediately before this experience, you were saying to me that you were glad you had made certain decisions, such as the one that you should seek me out."

The disciple was completely silent. But the farm worker said:

"I know you dervishes. You are trying to impress this hapless youth with your powers, but it is sure to be a form of trickery."

The obvious problem for the psychotherapeutic approach is that it so often attempts to "make sense" out of inherently senseless data. There is too often an inappropriate activation of reduced "rational" explanation according to the particular doctrine or theory taught. A rational, personal theory, as in this story, can almost always be constructed to make a coherent case out of a situation, centered on the actions and the importance of the "lower" self, as it is often termed in esoteric tradition.

It is often written within esoteric tradition that one does not build up the "ego," or self, nor does one destroy it, but merely keeps it out of the area of the particular teaching. This is often termed "alignment." It allows a full expression of the ordinary self, of reason and emotion in ordinary life. Here, then, is one pragmatic reason for the traditional separation of portions of esoteric instruction and practice from the remainder of a person's social, emotional, and professional life, the need for an area of human development to be kept "sacred," away from the reductionism of self-indulgence. This practice has been externally marked, in the past, by the designation of special "safe" places, cathedrals or temples; by the donning of special robes and hats or the like; and by such practices as leaving one's shoes at the door of the temple. These practices are all intended to suggest that one should "leave ordinary ideas and ordinary self out of this situation." This process is especially difficult, I find, for those interested in psychotherapy, growth, and encounter, since their training strengthens the ordinary person-centered assessment of situations, even those involving consciousness-development. These difficulties are the occasion for the continual stress in esoteric tradition on service and on humility, as a counter to self-preoccupation.

In an article entitled "What Sort of Awakening?" an anonymous writer in the October 30, 1974, issue of the excellent journal *MANAS* strikes the correct note:

. . . It should be plain enough that we need a moral order for our lives before we make much progress in the direction of individual power and control. It is for this reason, no doubt, that in the teachings of the Buddha, the ethical takes precedence over the acquisition of powers. The service of others, the purification of desire, the elimination of selfishness, come first for the greatest of the teachers of mankind. Would anyone seriously want to exchange a world filled with half-taught Yaqui magicians for even our world of self-satisfied and convention-bound technologists—intriguing as the idea may be? Or prefer a planetary archipelago of communes managed by self-preoccupied followers of Gurdjieff? Issues of "reality" are not involved here so much as the welfare of the human race—its need for the heroic service of a Prometheus, the self-sacrifice of a Christ, the universal compassion of a Buddha.

Meanwhile, the great resistance is progressing, the new ideas of man and nature are taking root, and the soil of inward discovery is becoming fertile again. It is much that we are trying to take command of our own lives, and finding good and sufficient reasons for thinking that we can and should. But, gaining command, what then will we *do* with our lives? Will we elaborate a more sophisticated hedonism, and start making all the old mistakes again, this time at a higher and more lethal level? Or will we, long before reaching the summit of independent decision, think deeply on what should be our meaning *for* the world?

In another story from *The Magic Monastery,* two men discuss the relationship of service to conscious development:

The Iranian asked: "And after you had perfected your service did the Baba confide his teachings in you?"

Hamid said: "As soon as I was able to serve, I was able to understand."

IV

Three generations have passed since Sigmund Freud shocked his contemporaries by propounding psychoanalysis in

Vienna, and touched off our own growth industries of psychotherapies, counseling, sexual seminars, and emotional-release institutes. It is not entirely coincidental that this century has also been a time in which the traditional perspective and understanding of human nature and human life have been reduced and often subverted by a search for a hidden "depth psychology," for a stable, "rational" personality on constant guard against an irrational "unconscious." These "threats" may be of an emotional nature, or of an unacknowledged and unwarranted sexuality. The search for a coherent "self" has become the cult enterprise of our times, a palliative for those who might seek a more complete consciousness.

One of my hobbies is collecting stories that contain patterns of action outside their nominal realm of function. If we take the conventional Freudian symbolism of the snake for a dangerous sexuality, and the "unconscious" as a dark lower depth, we find in the following story from *Time* magazine an adequate summary of the results of three generations of psychiatroid mentation. Although it is not its original title, it might be called "The Ballad of Psychoanalysis."

> Fred P. Shields, 73, spotted a nest of copperheads one day last week in the 80-ft. well on his farm in Cheshire, Ohio, so he enlisted his 42-year-old son Fred D. and his 18-year-old grandson James to help kill them.
>
> They attached a hose to the exhaust pipe of their pick-up truck, stuck the hose into the well and filled it with carbon-monoxide. After a while, Shields lowered himself into the well to see if the snakes were really dead. When he failed to come out again, his son went in after him. When the second man failed to come out, the grandson went in. Rescuers from the sheriff's office retrieved the three men, all dead, apparently of carbon-monoxide poisoning, but they found no sign of any snakes.

5

The Believers
and the Blind

The Book in Turki

A would-be disciple went to Bahaudin.

The master was surrounded by thirty of his students, in a garden, after dinner.

The newcomer said, "I wish to serve you."

Bahaudin answered, "You can best serve me by reading my *Risalat* [Letters]."

"I have already done so," said the newcomer.

"If you had done so in reality and not in appearance, you would not have approached me in this manner," said Bahaudin.

He continued, "Why do you think that you are able to learn?"

"I am ready to study with you."

Bahaudin said, "Let the most junior Murid [disciple] stand up."

Anwari, who was sixteen years of age, rose to his feet.

"How long have you been with us?" asked El-Shah.

"Three weeks, O Murshid."

"Have I taught you anything?"

"I do not know."

"Do you think so?"

"I do not think so."

Bahaudin said to him:

"In this newcomer's satchel you will find a book of poems. Take it in your hand and recite the entire contents without mistake and without even opening it."

Anwari found the book. He did not open it, but said: "I
fear that it is in Turki."

Bahaudin said, "Recite it!"

Anwari did so, and as he finished the stranger became
more and more affected by this wonder—a book being read
without being opened by someone who did not know Turki.

Falling at the feet of Bahaudin, he begged to be admitted
to the Circle.

Bahaudin said, "It is this kind of phenomenon which
attracts you—while it still does, you cannot really benefit
from it. That is why, even if you have read my *Risalat*, you
have not really read it.

"Come back," he continued, "when you have read it as
this beardless boy has read it. It was only such study that
gave him the power to recite from a book which he had not
opened, and at the same time prevented him from groveling
in wonderment at the event."

—Idries Shah, *Wisdom of the Idiots*

The scientific study of parapsychology has been with us for
over a century, without making any impression on the mainstream of psychology or physics. There are several reasons for
this. Many orthodox scientists in psychology and related areas,
as a function of their dominant paradigm, have consistently
refused to consider any outside evidence. The great nineteenth-
century German physiologist Hermann von Helmholz, for instance, wrote that "Neither the evidence of my own senses, nor
the testimony of all the Fellows of the Royal Society" would
convince him of the truth of parapsychologic data. And, in the
March 1976 issue of the *Journal of the Institute of Electrical and
Electronic Engineers* a reviewer is quoted rejecting a paper in
parapsychology, saying, "This is the kind of thing I wouldn't
believe in even if it were true."

We do not normally pursue scientific investigation into
phenomena which we consider impossible. If I were to propose
an experiment in training gorillas to become peach trees, I do
not think much financial support would appear, nor could I

enlist anyone's enthusiastic help. This aspect of research difficulty is rarely reported; people do not inform themselves about
things they do not believe to be possible. When Neal Miller, the
distinguished Rockefeller University psychologist, first began his
research on the possibility of a voluntary control (by animals)
of certain "involuntary" processes such as blood flow and gastric
secretions, his research efforts were significantly slowed because
he could not find any graduate students who believed sufficiently
that such control was possible and who would work on the
subject.

Often, if sensory or conceptual information does not coin-
cide with our expectations, we ignore it. In a demonstration
experiment, Jerome Bruner presented groups of people with
quickly flashed photographs of playing cards. The ordinary cards
were easily identified, but "anomalous" ones, such as a red ace
of spades, were either ignored or were "corrected"—perceived
and reported as the black ace of spades or the ace of hearts.

This inherent conservatism in human perception is at its
peak in the scientific study of phenomena which are by definition unusual and challenging. Indeed, the claims of parapsychology are a distinct challenge to our contemporary psychological and physical world-views. If some people can perceive events
before they "happen" (or at least before the remainder of us
perceive them), if there are modes of interpersonal communication unknown to many, if people can influence action or events
at a distance greater than the range of normal influence, then
perhaps we should revise our conception of human abilities, of
seriality, of space and time, and of our conception of how events
become manifest. Since the burden of documentation is on those
who claim that these capacities exist, their contentions on the
nature of the mind and the physical world should be accepted
only after much evidence has been accumulated.

William James noted that the appearance of only one white
crow is needed to dispel forever the idea that all crows are
black. In an idealist's world this would certainly be true. But

we, however, must consider the subtlety in perceptual barriers which modern scientific research and clinical investigations have uncovered. We need much more evidence than one isolated experiment to overthrow (or radically extend) an accepted world-view. The existence of William James's poor white crow might well be dismissed by the Statistics Department as "statistically insignificant." One bit of Jamesian evidence ought to be enough, but is not. Each experiment stands or falls on probability estimates, not on any set of absolute criteria. We can, for instance, find many fragmentary bits of evidence, even in the daily newspapers, that events do not always occur as they "ought," and that quite improbable things happen. We don't for that reason consider them "paranormal," even though such consideration might well promote a more fluid concept of our surroundings. There is a conceptual link between the "improbable" and the "paranormal," despite the unfortunate distinction maintained by fanatics on both sides.

FISH KILLS SEAGULL

Brixham, England

Members of a yacht club say they saw a fish kill a seagull.

They said when the bird dived Wednesday to grab a fish in Brixham Harbor, the fish grabbed the seagull, pulled it beneath the water and drowned it.

United Press

SECRET MAPS

London

The British Defense Ministry ordered an investigation yesterday to determine how secret U.S. Air Force maps came to be used as wrapping paper by a London furniture company.

A Defense Ministry spokesman said the maps came here from Germany but he had no idea how.

They were first discovered and brought to the attention of British authorities by a Birmingham customer of the London company.

Associated Press

WIFE LANDS ON STRAYING HUSBAND

Prague

Vera Czermak jumped out of her third story window when she learned her husband had betrayed her.

Mrs. Czermak is recovering in the hospital after landing on her husband, who was killed, the newspaper *Vecerny Pravda* reported yesterday.

United Press

Many publicizers of parapsychology seek to counter their skeptics by proclamation. They insist that there is now a significant amount of incontrovertible scientific evidence in behalf of parapsychology. This is, I think, as unjustified as the orthodox reviewers' insistence that no evidence could possibly convince them.

After reading most of the available literature on parapsychology, and traveling to the major laboratories where research is being done, I can agree with neither the fanatic believers and promotionalists nor those who advocate blind rejection. It is obviously nonsense to maintain that a class of phenomena cannot *possibly* occur. Yet the opposite position, that the "field" of parapsychology is stable and mature and needs but a minor filling-in of data in several research areas (an experiment or two in telepathy, clairvoyance, etc.), is hardly any more justified by the evidence or by the theoretical accomplishments of parapsychologists.

It is fair to demand that theories and research evidence in this area of investigation be of the highest quality, and positive results reproduced by others at their convenience. Otherwise we should have to take the word of a minor group of investigators, many of whom are more interested in popular acclaim than in scientific study.

Unfortunately, most contemporary theories in parapsychology are simply laughable. Uri Geller, following the Unidentified-Flying-Object theoretical approach, claims that a "flying saucer" sends him information on an internal TV set. Astronaut-turned-popularizer Edgar Mitchell, in his *Psychic Exploration,* lags not far behind. His theory seems to consist entirely of the incantation "Outerspace, Innerspace," as in "we've conquered outer space, now let's do inner space," a theme echoed by many of his contributors. On a supposedly more serious level, there are pseudo-physics-parapsychological activities which range from the cultivation of supposed "faster-than-light experiences" with a partner to interminable analyses of the confused statements of physicists, mystics, and parapsychologists on the nature of reality. The recurrent theme seems to be that Modern Physics finds many phenomena incomprehensible, as do parapsychologists. Therefore, these disciplines must be (a) similar and (b) on to something.*

In view of the tradition of poor theory and irresponsible speculation, we should require that writers and researchers in this area exhibit a far greater degree of trustworthiness and lucidity than in other areas of scientific investigation, simply because a positive outcome in parapsychological experiments would have great consequences. If an experiment in "verbal learning," or in animal maze work, does not "replicate," there is no great upheaval, no consternation in the public press, since there is little of conceptual import at stake. The case is different with parapsychology. Experiments are subject to such scrutiny that we had the sorry sight of the Stanford Research Institute's research reports on Uri Geller debunked before anyone had seen them. In a recent magazine article, two scientists were quoted regarding some of the preliminary procedures of these experiments, without it being noted that they had not observed an actual experiment. In any research, there is a period of "setting up"—successive attempts to approximate a final, formal experiment. This is a period in which researchers are free to try out alternative approaches. It is perfectly legitimate, a valid

---

* I refer the reader to Laurence Le Shan's *The Medium, the Mystic, and the Physicist* (Viking, 1973), and to Arthur Koestler's *The Roots of Coincidence* (Harper & Row, 1972) for this last approach.

part of doing an experiment and, since the procedure of "setting up" is never made public, forms a useful function. No one can fairly criticize a scientific report simply because some of the unreported preliminaries do not satisfy a visiting investigator.

Since parapsychology has been largely dominated by two warring camps, the ardent Believers and the determined Blind, it is not surprising that both groups have been guilty of excesses. In 1974, J. Levy of Duke University was operating the laboratory of J. B. Rhine, the founder of American scientific parapsychology. Levy had published a series of well-received articles on parapsychology, demonstrating the ability of animals to avoid random shock by precognition. Details of the sophisticated randomizer were published, and many inquirers were told that this research would be among the first to demonstrate a repeatable parapsychological experiment. Levy's experiments were technically sophisticated, automatic in operation, and "honestly" repeatable, because he used animals (supposedly beyond influence). Levy was, in fact, caught cheating by his peers. He had set the automatic, "unbiased" recording apparatus to yield far more correct choices by the animals than they'd actually made. This was a damaging blow to the whole field of parapsychology, since its empiric basis is so slight.

There was a similar scandal at the Sloan-Kettering Institute, also in 1974. A dermatologist there faked the relevant evidence on the possibility of transplanting skin grafts, which is thought by immunologists to be impossible. Like Levy's, his career was ruined. Few people discredit responsible inquiry in skin-transplant immunology because of the Sloan-Kettering scandal. But parapsychology, on the other hand, is highly susceptible to the sort of self-defeating blunder made by Dr. Levy. Another difference is that the world of parapsychology contains within it quite a large number of untrained and inadequate workers, who claim much merely on the basis of their belief.

For a real scientific study of phenomena mistakenly called "parapsychological" or "paranormal," we shall need a steady accumulation of high-quality evidence from independent sources, evidence repeatable by others and linked with adequate predictive and theoretical justification. One or two isolated experiments will not suffice. To return to James: If there exists, indeed, a single white crow, then to the very few people who have seen it, all crows are no longer black. But to the community at large *it would not mean very much* because the reports of the white crow would be too few and too unsupported to be of any practical consequence. Contemporary evidence in parapsychology falls between the stools: it is neither too insignificant to be completely ignored, nor is it developed sufficiently to be of real impact.

To investigate the area, we must first consider those who are professionally involved in gathering evidence and communicating research. It must be admitted that parapsychology harbors more than its share of publicists masquerading as scientists, those who are simply incompetent, those who may be competent in business technology or space flight and therefore assume they are competent in parapsychology, those who find in these nether and sometimes spooky regions of thought a tenuous connection with a degenerated mysticism, and those who are simply trying to make a name for themselves.

Since there is no training in responsible investigation in this area, research parapsychologists do not come from the same scientific population as those in psychology or physics. They tend, unfortunately, to be of the fringe or flake element, with the advantages and drawbacks of that position. They are regarded suspiciously by the mainstream, sometimes unjustly, yet at the same time receive the acclaim of talk-show and after-dinner audiences, and appear in print much more than their work merits. This complete rejection/adulation syndrome is similar to that of a belief in any sect and an attempt to scientize that belief. A good example is the proponents of the current ideologically based research, done almost exclusively by believers, "proving" that Transcendental Meditation is Good For You.

Keeping all these difficulties in mind, let us consider the current status of research in paranormal phenomena. One problem for the responsible researcher or theorist is the lack of a sufficiently repeatable experiment. Early research in England as well as in the United States was devoted to the creation of a repeatable research program which could be employed by many investigators to test unusual psychic ability. There are many remnants of the research of this era—"ESP cards," specially constructed dice, matching figures, exciting tests of sensitives and mediums—some fraudulent, some not. But most reviewers agree that the early experiments did not yield much save the idea that research in this area could be conducted expertly, with honor, and that very minor fragments of unusual evidence could be uncovered at great effort. The yield, however, as in a mine worked with obsolete techniques, was too slight to impress the mainstream researchers in psychology or the general public.

More contemporary workers have attempted to consider phenomena more carefully. Under what conditions might these unusual experiences occur? To whom? Can people be trained to increase their perceptions? Are there more subtle research measures which might more consistently index these functions? Measures which might increase the yield? If parapsychology is to become part of the scientific investigation of man, it is these questions it must pursue. I have chosen to examine several investigators, or groups of them, in order to emphasize a few subtle and potentially rewarding directions of research.

One of the most publicized recent parapsychological investigations was the research of Harold Puthoff and Russell Targ at the Stanford Research Institute in Menlo Park, California. Most, if not all, of the publicity and controversy surrounded their investigation of Uri Geller, the showman Israeli "psychic." It is difficult for me to understand why Geller has received the attention he has save for the public interest—and publicity distortions—of this field of investigation. Geller has certainly achieved one aim: he is famous. He has been on every TV chat

show in the world, he has made the cover of the British magazine *New Scientist*. He has been portrayed in *Psychology Today*
as both a psychic and a fraud, based on an extremely casual investigation by Andrew Weil. Uri Geller has "made it," but only
in the public-relations realm of "I don't care what you say, so
long as you spell my name right."

The Stanford Research Institute investigators initially
worked with Geller in the hope of obtaining a repeatable experiment, one that other laboratories could replicate. With such a
"talented subject," they hoped that many phenomena which
might be below threshold in ordinary people could be easily produced, repeated, and analyzed. The hopes were not met. Geller
proved extremely difficult to work with, and the experiments
were not of much import. Those published did not involve psy-
chokinesis, which is Geller's claim to fame ("psychic watch-re-
pair," etc.), but picture-drawing experiments in which Geller,
inside a sealed room, reproduced the contents of pictures outside, and quite a good match was reported. But since Geller is
more a creature of the media than a serious subject of science,
his antics are best left to the Sunday supplements and their
readers, who have often focused on the pseudo-question, "Is he
real or a fraud?" The possibility that he may be both genuine
and a fraud is unsatisfying to both the Believers and the Blind.

It is often overlooked that even if Geller were, as claimed,
"the greatest psychic ever to reach these shores," he still would
yield little in the way of useful evidence of "psychic powers"
in ordinary people. Geller is, by his own definition, unusual, and
at best would display only tantalizing possibilities, which would
need much follow-up with less extreme subjects and procedures.

Partly because of the difficulties of working with eccentrics
and partly because of the need to round out a research program
with more relevance to normal people, the SRI researchers' most
potentially interesting evidence comes from a series of initial
pilot studies of "remote viewing."

Remote viewing is described as the ability to perceive objects and events from a distance, objects not present in any conventionally defined sense. Such ability is often described in religious tradition and in esoteric studies. The SRI researchers have concentrated on this area because they considered it a more primary use of extraordinary ability than card-guessing and other more mechanical tasks. The latter may be better subject to quantification, but are probably further away from any potential evolutionary advantage. I think this is a useful approach of these researchers: to consider situations which could be survival-related, in evolutionary terms, and adapt the experiments to the situation. The alternative has been to wind up precisely quantifying little of any real import, as had Rhine. However, the SRI researchers pay the price of producing uncontrolled experiments, experiments which are, more correctly, preliminary investigations.

To deal with such "real life" situations is more complex than an experiment whose outcome can always be predicted by precise laws of chance. How can we estimate the role of chance in guessing a certain event, or a person's presence? The concept of chance is something that many ordinary people, and even statistics-trained social scientists, often misinterpret—all that the derived odds yield is what ought to happen to an object, say a bouncing ball, over eons if the same functions were repeated. On any one run, all we can do is assign probabilities that one event may happen. In a billion runs, we would expect a "one-in-a-billion" shot. Similarly, the "Laws of Physics," often ill-defined, are said to be "impossible to violate" by such phenomena as precognition and telepathy. This is nonsense, since contemporary physics is, again, statistical, and its boundaries are the few things which *cannot* occur. It does not describe a formal set of conditions which are intimately predictive. This means, I submit, that modern quantum and relativistic physics are irrelevant to, and their value is unshaken by, the success or failure of parapsychology, the publicists of a "paraphysics" notwithstanding. That what happened to the seagull and the fish, in the example quoted above, is improbable does not render it impossible. Its improbability might cause us to ignore it if we were present, yet, in more defined situations, we would not ignore a high-jumper who can cross the bar at a new world-record height simply because a random selection of college juniors would not perform as well.

The SRI studies are tentative and investigative, and should be considered initial, sometimes quite imperfect, attempts to define the area of inquiry, and not as formal Euclidian proofs of the existence of anything in particular. They are interesting "pilot studies."

The published research on "remote viewing" consists primarily of work with a second subject, Pat Price, a former California Police Commissioner and now a business executive. Price volunteered himself to the SRI group as a subject, since he was interested in his ability to perceive objects at a distance. He is quite modest and unassuming, not in the least interested in notoriety or publicity.

The remote-viewing experiments follow a similar pattern. One of the SRI experimenters opens a set of previously prepared "traveling descriptions" that outline a trip to a chosen site somewhere in the San Francisco Bay Area. These "traveling descriptions" are prepared by someone not otherwise associated with the experiment. Thirty minutes are given for the actual trip to the site, and a signal is given by walkie-talkie that the experimenters have arrived. Pat Price is then asked to describe the site. Only after the description is taken is information on the actual site given to Price. Again, it would be difficult to assign a simple probability to his guessing correctly, since people's descriptions of the same place and the same event may differ widely. For this reason a set of judges are asked to visit the nine sites chosen for the Price experiment and to match, blindly, the descriptions given by Price with the sites as they experienced them. This preserves both the naturalistic quality of the experiment and the judging, and does yield a probability estimate, since by chance the judges should guess only one of the nine correctly. The matches were quite above what one would expect.

Targ and Puthoff have continued their work. They have tried their remote-viewing research on several other subjects, and even go so far as to claim that almost anyone can perform remote viewing if the situation is set up correctly. In one experiment, the object was a tennis match. The subject drew it tolerably, if not artistically. But when asked to *describe* what he saw, he reported a restaurant scene, with people seated at tables, eating. Here, as in many other aspects of parapsychology, it seems that the overall picture is remotely available and the words are not. In looking at the picture he had drawn, the subject misinterpreted the scene, although it was fairly accurate pictorially. The information was present, that is, but not at the level of verbal consciousness.

These experiments raise the possibility of there being different modes of information transmission. Information may reach an intuitive, symbolic, or pictorial awareness, yet may not be expressible in words. Since we identify consciousness with verbal expression, our idea about the availability of information regarding an event may be at times incorrect. If this analysis is reasonable, then these remote perceptual abilities might be very widely distributed indeed—yet they might not reach full verbal awareness in most people. In a controlled experiment, detection of information transmission could be done by sensitive physiological indices which might yield a means of measurement repeatable over a wide variety of subjects. The SRI researchers and others are pursuing this line by means of EEG and other measures. They report a tentative initial success with one person.

Perhaps we might loosely consider these so-called paranormal abilities merely dormant, and untrained within our culture, yet they might be detected with more sensitive indexing as in biofeedback training. If so, there may be vestiges of such receptivity available for study by sophisticated means, even though individuals may not have the "conscious" (that is, verbal) ability to recognize them. As I mentioned, the experiment is at best a pilot effort and first needs repetition in other laboratories, perhaps with an initial selection of subjects who are disposed to believe in their abilities. If early tests are successful, later experiments might delineate the personality characteristics of successful subjects and might sort people by measures such as hypnotic susceptibility, and other personality characteristics. The SRI researchers do not satisfy all objections, but they have opened interesting areas of work.

At the University of California at Davis, Professor Charles T. Tart has conducted a series of studies which investigate another possibility of bringing intuitive performance up to a higher level so that it might be more consistently studied. In the past several years, we have seen that many previously scoffed-at "paranormal" faculties can be trained if the appropriate feedback information is given. If I had stated, as recently as fifteen years ago, that the claims of Yoga masters to cease heart pumping and to reduce blood pressure might be valid, I would have been considered a fool. Now, such subtle physiological phenomena are well verified, and college sophomores at several universities are even invited to learn to raise and lower blood pressure and heart rate as part of their introduction to psychology. In addition, such functions as muscle potential and brain electrical function can be regulated if given proper "feedback." Tart applies the same ideals to parapsychology, employing immediate feedback devices to train his subjects to make correct choices not ordinarily considered possible.

One training device that is semicommercially available is a four-choice trainer. Subjects are asked to guess which of a series of choices will light up on the following trial. If the system is calibrated for frequency and for transition probability (e.g., we might have a system which displays each of four choices 25 percent of the time, but often follows a certain ordering such as

1–3–4–2, or we might find that 2 follows 1 with greater frequency than chance, etc.), we would guess that responses would be at chance level.

If individuals can obtain immediate feedback on their performance, can they, in a manner similar to that of biofeedback training, learn to associate internal cues (here, of being correct) with the outcome? Targ and Puthoff attempted a similar study with little success. Tart found little success with the four-choice trainer and attempted to use a ten-choice machine in addition in his study. He felt that a ten-choice trainer (TCT) would be of more interest since the chance of being falsely reinforced for ESP in the four-choice was 25 percent, here only 10 percent.

In his experiment, Tart sought to give the subjects all the "legal" encouragement possible. The target lights are circular on the TCT, and, while the subjects attempted to guess the proper position, they were observed by the experimenter, who had himself chosen the target on that trial. Indeed, to facilitate this, the chosen spot was lit on the TV monitor which the experimenter viewed. The experimenter was isolated from the subject but could watch on a television monitor, and he reported becoming quite involved in "influencing" the subject's choice through the same sort of body English that spectators use at a sports event.

Tart's TCT experiment is another potential paradigm for repeatable research in this area. Yet the subjects in his own experiment did *not*, it seems, learn to greatly improve their intuitive abilities. Instead, there were a group of people who entered the experiment with some ability to perform better than chance, and who continued to do so throughout the experiment, and a very few who might have improved. This is in contrast to many previous experiments in which, without immediate feedback, the subject's performance degraded with time. Tart may have developed a measure that could stabilize performance, if repeated, although the early results are disappointing.

At Maimonides Medical Center in Brooklyn a third series of experiments is in progress which considers another aspect of the problem, the "state of consciousness" of the subject while "receiving" information in an unusual manner. The original series of these experiments was done under the direction of Montague Ullman, with help from other colleagues such as Robert Van Der Castle, Charles Honorton, and Stanley Krippner. These experiments involve dreams. One subject sleeps, and while he is in a Rapid-Eye-Movement (REM) period, his partner attempts to "project" images chosen at random by experimenters.

When the REM period ends, the sleeping subject is awakened and quizzed about his experience during the dream. His description is, again, blind-judged against the stimulus material by people unfamiliar with the experiment. In a few cases the matches have been good, and this research has attracted interest because of its design and theoretical sophistication. But the results have not been repeated, and, like the other two experiments cited, Dr. Ullman's should be considered only potentially interesting early studies, but still, studies which consider another important point, the state of the subject during the experiment.

Charles Honorton, who has now taken over the Ullman laboratory, is refining the method. He now asks his subjects to look through a "Ganzfeld," a set of half ping-pong balls, which is intended to provide homogeneous visual input. He then asks his subjects to listen to "white noise" in order to mask auditory input. These masking devices are used to eliminate the ordinary sensory distractions that might interfere with this unusual manner of perception. As with the dream studies, the Ganzfeld-wearer attempts to receive information on a randomly chosen target "sent" or "projected" by a second subject in a remote room. The preliminary results are intriguing and show that, in some cases, unusual aspects of information transmission occur, but again, they have not been repeated by anyone else and should be before any further speculations are made.

To assess the status of research and theorizing in parapsychology is obviously difficult. I think, though, that the time both of the Believers and the Blind is over. Parapsychology—actually, it might be called, more accurately, "intuition training"—may *not* be an idea whose "time has come," as some of its publicity-seeking apologists claim, but it *is* time to give this study its due. It is a field in which there are enough developed research procedures and suggestive bits of evidence on the nature of information transmission, on the possibility of training, on the state of consciousness of those involved—enough for a few responsible investigators to perform a sufficient number of dispassionate scientific experiments. They might even eventually hope to settle many of the ancient questions and to dispel some of the fantasies of the gullible as well as the skepticism of the hyper-rationalists. To take a legal analogy, there is enough suggestive evidence to justify a fair trial, free from the lunatics who have pressed for it inappropriately, and free from the summary rejection of many. Its scientific study must go beyond the camps of the Believers and the Blind. Parapsychology deserves at least its "day in court"—if for no other reason than its potential to bring us closer to a perception of our evolutionary development.

6

A Lesson of Carlos Castaneda

People have looked to parapsychology as a substitute for their own experience, as others have turned to psychotherapy and its "growth center" derivatives. There are those who have sought escapism through drugs and exotic experiences, and adulate writers like Carlos Castaneda while missing much of their serious import. Here I consider Castaneda's primary—his first—lesson.

For many, "the entry into another world," a radical extension of their consciousness, never comes, despite all their longing. For a few, it comes as part of a difficult but nonetheless contemporary discipline. For fewer still, it is doubly difficult, a development of awareness combined with an attempt to reconstruct completely a social consciousness based on Western sensibilities. Carlos Castaneda is one of the third group, along with those who have traveled to Tibet or to Mecca, or tried to convert to the Japanese form of Zen. In these instances a dual journey is required: one of consciousness, one of re-socialization. If the second is unnecessary, it is nonetheless adventurous and exciting.

Castaneda's books are popular in part because of their exotic nature, in part because he is a fine writer, and in part because of the dramatic, cinematic quality of his adventure story. His books are important, less for their superb portrayal of the mind and potential of the Sonora Shaman, "Don Juan," than for their outline of the many obstacles over which a Western intellectual needs to pass in order to enter and personally incorporate an alien culture.

I will not attempt to write a lengthy summary of Castaneda's introduction to peyote, and the rituals surrounding it,
and his later understanding that drugs were not the end point
of his journey. In those discoveries, his own experiences parallel
many others. Also, the question of whether his four books are
totally fiction, totally reportage, or a mixture of both is irrelevant to the lesson of Carlos Castaneda, since what is most
interesting is what he communicates himself, not what he attributes to another. As with Rafael Lefort's *The Teachers of
Gurdjieff*, Castaneda's books represent the failure of a rational,
verbal, sequential approach to comprehend matters of esoteric
tradition, and in Castaneda's case, to integrate fully the two
modes of knowledge.

Sometimes an apprenticeship or study with a person of an
alien culture leaves one exhilarated, extended in consciousness,
yet not integrated. On my own travels to Bali in Indonesia, for
instance, I was at times so transfixed by the surroundings, the
music, the overpowering smell of a mixture of urine, sweat, and
roasting *satih*, and by the terrible heat that I could only alternate
between completely doubting my surroundings and an inability
to conceive that people in New York were going about their
daily activities at that same moment. And thus is Castaneda
able, by great struggle with his admittedly overdramatic self,
to enter into and participate in the world of the Indian Shaman;
and thus, too, does he remain unable to integrate his experiences
and to bring them home to our society. In Castaneda's case,
a stray teaching is found, entered at double the effort, and yet
it is not integrated.

I do not attempt to slight the achievement in either the
research or the writing of these books, but rather to begin
to consider Castaneda's work with neither the summary rejection of the mainstream academic nor the uncritical acceptance
of the sensation-seeking audience which he never sought. Castaneda's attempt is dual, at the same time spiritual and anthropological. For the anthropologist, his work succeeds in entering

an alien construction of the world, thereby exemplifying and bringing home the point that our ordinary consciousness, what we consider our "world," is a construction, our *idea* of the world. But this is a far cry from the conventional armchair anthropologist's academic reduction of the various "ideas of the world" held by diverse societies to "cultural relativism." Castaneda is able to dramatize aspects of this alternate mode in graphic personal detail. As wild as this particular world may be, it forever demonstrates to the reader the alternate realities, not only of place but of consciousness, available to men of differing societies.

Considered as a potentially useful spiritual teaching, however, Castaneda's work lacks a developed organic connection with contemporary life. To transpose the situation: on a pleasure trip, one might travel to a Central American jungle and experience extraordinary rare plants, yet those exotic flora cannot be taken home intact and grown in North America, in a more "civilized" temperate climate. The exotic plants fade, and will not thrive when transplanted. Thus Castaneda, for all his fame, has wisely not set up a "school" of instant mysticism or a cult based on himself or his Yaqui Shaman friends.

There are many personally affecting aspects of Castaneda's work, such as the poignant and dramatic ending of *Journey to Ixtlan*, and a scene at a posh restaurant in Mexico City, in *Tales of Power*, both of them notable for their remarkable visual qualities. Yet to me, the most important lesson of Carlos Castaneda's work is contained on the very first page of his first book, *The Teachings of Don Juan: A Yaqui Way of Knowledge*. It consists of an account of events on June 23, 1961. He writes:

My notes on my first session with Don Juan are dated June 23, 1961. That was the occasion when the teachings began. I had seen him several times previously in the capacity of an observer only. At every opportunity I had asked him to teach me about peyote. He ignored my request every time, but he never completely dismissed the subject, and I inter-

preted his hesitancy as a possibility that he might be in-
clined to talk about his knowledge with more coaxing.

In this particular session he made it obvious to me that
he might consider my request provided I possessed clarity
of mind and purpose in reference to what I had asked him.
It was impossible for me to fulfill such a condition, for I
had asked him to teach me about peyote only as a means of
establishing a link of communication with him. I thought
his familiarity with the subject might predispose him to be
more open and willing to talk, thus allowing me an entrance
into his knowledge on the properties of plants. He had
interpreted my request literally, however, and was concerned about my purpose in wishing to learn about peyote.

Here he mentions having met "Don Juan" several times
before but, with his Western analytic, academic reductionist
mentality, he has completely missed what he has been previously
taught. In this quite carefully considered first book, Castaneda
has ignored, and does not even mention, the intense training in
personal development which Don Juan had previously offered
him, and which he later determines to be the main line of the
teachings available to him. He is initially fixated, focused on
drugs and on the "experience" which he hopes to receive, and he
misses the esoteric teaching.

The account published four years later in *Journey to Ixtlan*
corrects the record, and Castaneda recognizes and now includes
the teachings given him before June 23, 1961, when he had
previously considered that "the teachings began." He, like most
of us trained in the West, had been unable to recognize spiritual teaching even when it was directly presented to him, and even
when it required his own strenuous efforts. Many of us, however interested in these areas, often fail to perceive the important elements of esoteric traditions. We usually are searching for
our own preconceptions, be they the "drug high," "the miraculous," ancient rituals, or "experiences of consciousness." Castaneda was given information on and specific exercises for "eras-

ing personal history," learning to upset the ordinary social matrix of appointments/expectations in which most of us are held. He was invited to attain some degree of the humility ("losing self-importance") necessary to attempt to understand the role of death in his own life and to assume responsibility for that life. These "lessons" are often considered preparatory to involvement in many more advanced forms of esoteric tradition. Castaneda was being offered the basics of an extended knowledge but, like most of us, completely ignored them, focused as he was on the "drug experience" at the time, as many have been, yet we currently look to meditation, or to instant experiences, gymnastic exotic postures, or ancient and lofty "systems."

Castaneda's experience demonstrates primarily that the Western-trained intellectual, even a "seeker," is by his culture almost completely unprepared to understand esoteric traditions. Castaneda is unsparing of himself in all four of his books on this point. We do not often realize that such an extended knowledge cannot be instantly transferred or even "given" in one experience,* but demands a radical change in our attitude toward our lives, though not necessarily in the external fate of our lives. No hopeful journeys to Central or South America are really necessary, nor voyages to the Middle or Far East, or Africa. We do not attain an extended consciousness by an instant cultural transplant, by a sentimental journey to other cultures, by adopting the habits of an ancient tradition, or the dress of the Indian holy man.

In Castaneda's 1972 retelling of that most important day, June 23, 1961, Don Juan mentions the teachings previously offered.

> As soon as I sat down I bombarded Don Juan with questions. He did not answer me and made an impatient gesture with his hand to be quiet. He seemed to be in a serious mood.

---

* Here Castaneda's early, unrealized, and mistaken hope for peyote.

"I was thinking that you haven't changed at all in the time you've been trying to learn about plants," he said in an accusing tone.

He began reviewing in a loud voice all the changes of personality he had recommended I should undertake.

Castaneda writes, "I told him that I had considered the matter very seriously and found that I could not possibly fulfill them because each of them ran contrary to my core."

7

Caveat Meditator

For many people, the first experiences of an extended consciousness have come from newly organized groups. Some of these
groups are resolutely commercial, others clannish and secretive. In
considering both types of groups, we encounter, again, the difficulties of understanding and conveying an advanced knowledge
of human capacities. In observing how these "franchised mysticism
groups" promote and maintain themselves, we can note how the
original knowledge seems to shrink to fit commercial requirements.

I

Many people have been associated with both psychotherapy and
parapsychology for many years. The advent of trademarked,
franchised mystic cults, however, is a more recent development.
Some people seize upon them as the latest stage in their own
continual self-preoccupation and indulgence; others seek new
"experiences" for themselves. Such forms of meditation, and of
awareness-training, have usually met with immediate and continued disdain from professional psychologists and educators,
sometimes justified, sometimes for the wrong reasons. That these
pop cults and organizations exist and thrive is in large part due
to the same lag in mainstream awareness that has allowed the
psychotherapeutic disciplines to extend their rightful role in our
affairs. Along with our cultivation of intellectual skills, and the

increasing prominence of those skills in education and professional life (with attendant specialization of function), there has been an almost complete abdication of teachings regarding the person and what could be called wisdom and self-knowledge. The trademarked awareness systems have, therefore, moved into an area of "applied psychology" in disuse within the academic and educational professions.

The systems offer either one special technique or a synthetic amalgam of techniques drawn from many sources. These techniques, in spite of the opinion of most academics, may not be entirely worthless. The "systems" do continue the fragmentation and degeneration of an authentic mystical tradition. Although the piecemeal benefits of these cults may be of scattered and transient use, such benefits are often perverted to the perpetration and dominance of the system, or to the personal service and material benefit of the leader. The process is similar to the bureaucratic encrustation of a new and perhaps useful government program: the original impetus is lost. If quite important traditional teachings about the person and conscious evolution have fallen into the hands of the contemporary guru-superstar industry, then both the organizers of this industry and those responsible for our education share responsibility. After all, if one is denied normal food one will search out alternatives, even food that makes one sick.

In our society, where is one to learn how to calm one's mind in times of stress, how to improve personal relationships, attain a measure of responsibility for the direction of one's life, and come to terms with one's own creation of experience of the world, let alone an intuitive wisdom of the purpose of life? The existence of "instant-weekend" and simpleminded meditation-training systems tells us more about what is missing from contemporary education, even at a rudimentary level, than any amount of professional criticism could do—we are a society of spiritual illiterates, suckers for a quick answer. Many have turned to the showmen/salesmen and to the recycled Indian dropout to make up for the basic shortcomings of our education —and at great, and often unnecesary, cost.

We are lax in the training of personal knowledge. We may spend years perfecting our tennis stroke, yet precious little training is offered on the nature of our bodies or on the personal dimensions of our own experience. Much modern research, for instance, shows our ordinary consciousness to be a *construction* of the world, a "best guess" about the nature of reality. Yet rarely, if ever, in psychology or education classes is this fact brought home to students and made part of their experience. Rarely are students acquainted with procedures that might allow them to realize the benefits of this understanding. "Academic" learning is rather determinedly kept in one sphere, with its own professionals and hierarchy, "applied" training in another: rarely does the academic become involved in training people, and rarely does the "applied" pychologist or educator make any dent in mainstream academic thinking.

The new, franchised self-improvement courses are neither the instant self-transcendence–fantastic-enlightenment panaceas that their followers resolutely contend, nor are they, as most academics contend, entirely lacking any phenomena of interest. Most self-awareness programs provide some of the rudiments of a once-complete technology of consciousness. In the absence of anything more highly developed, such programs impress their followers, and yield great benefits to their leaders—after all, a simple tape recorder might be enough to convince a primitive tribe that the bearer was a representative of the deity. From one system, one can learn to relax; from a second, to relate; from a third, to respond. Converts are often attained by classic methods: program leaders offer either a minor service to the inexperienced in the meditation/relaxation system, for example, or they offer a severe initiation/conversion experience, as in the large-scale awareness-training systems. Particular systems come and go, inspired, perhaps, by a given site or the particular style of a leader or a particular technique, yet their successes and excesses remain fairly constant.

Consider one such reduced example of a complete tradition: the practices of meditation as developed in various cultures of the world and in various cultural eras are quite diverse. The practice may involve whirling, chanting, singing, or concentration on the movement of the breath, on specially posed questions, or on an internal sound. It may consist solely of ordinary activities, imbued with "mindfulness"; it may involve prayer in the church, in quiescence, or in unison. There may be an attempt to deliberately separate two coexistent streams of consciousness. Other, more advanced techniques may involve the control of various "centers" in the body, as in early Christian mysticism, and receptivity to communications beyond the norm. Meditation practices have many, many diverse functions, depending on the nature of the students and of the society.

The primary function of the diverse techniques of meditation is to begin to answer the basic questions of life, such questions as go unanswered in ordinary social or educational interaction. For instance, one might ask, "What is the purpose of existence?" or "What is death?" in the same verbal analytic mode as one might ask, "What is the size of that building?" Most of us are trained to ask questions in this manner. But those of esoteric tradition contend that personal questions about the nature of existence cannot be answered in the same rational, verbal manner as can questions about the nature of the physical or even social environment. Meditation, then, is "a-logical," intended to defeat the ordinary sequential and analytic approach to problem-solving in situations where this approach is not appropriate.

Questions are sometimes given that have no answer, for the purpose of showing, simply, that not all questions that can be posed can be answered. A Zen Master might ask, "What is the size of the real you?"—then instruct a follower to return with the answer, an answer obviously impossible to express in words or in rational thought. One *koan,* as such questions are called, is the following: "If you say this stick is real, I will beat you with it. If you say this stick is not real, I will beat you with it. If you do not say anything at all, I will beat you with it." Obviously, this is a situation in which there is little one can *say,* since the appropriate response lies in another realm.

A Japanese academic who wished to "understand" Zen more fully went to a monastery to submit himself to the koans. He was asked "What is *mu?*"—to define, that is, a word which has no meaning in Japanese. As a good scholar, he proceeded to look up the syllable in Japanese and other Oriental dictionaries to determine a potential root meaning and habitual usage. He presented his findings to the Master, who repulsed him and immediately sent him away. Our scholar next thought the question to be more subtle and tried to analyze the tonal component of the syllable in every language of the Chinese group. He again presented his findings to the Master, who now thought it was time to convince this poor scholar of the seriousness of his situation, that it was not a question of another academic excursion. "I will give you one more chance," he said, "and if you do not solve the riddle, I will cut off your leg." Now, even in the most extreme arguments or thesis examinations of the academic world, things usually don't become this rough. But the threat did frighten the scholar "out of his wits," so to speak. He completely concentrated upon the syllable itself, trying to puzzle out the meaning, and in the process of concentration itself he achieved the result. The question had a nonanalytic effect, and a nonverbal result as well. Those who are not privy to the extreme concentration brought about by the Zen Master's exercise, or the scholar's reply, might not realize that many of the most important and compelling questions that face us cannot be looked up in an encyclopedia or dictionary. There is no place where the meaning of one's life is "written up."

Chanting, whirling, and other exercises are concentration

techniques, exercises whose primary effect is mental, not confined to mere relaxation or to a highly promoted "fourth state of consciousness" involving deep relaxation. That we become confused when considering meditation is partly due to the fact that many of the undeveloped esoteric traditions come to us mixed with their Indian, Japanese, and Middle Eastern backgrounds, with their particular medical and cosmological systems and other cultural trappings. It is again a problem of the container and the content—we cannot sufficiently distinguish those aspects of esoteric tradition which can be important for the development of our own consciousness from the less importable foreign aspects of cultural style. Vegetarianism, for instance, is widespread and is functional in India due to the short supply of meat (which, when available, is often of poor quality, or even dangerous). Similarly, speaking Japanese, or using soy sauce (or, better, Tamari) is no more "spiritual" than consuming hot dogs, ketchup, or beer. Not useful either is the wholesale adaptation of a particular system of Indian medicine or cosmology, when in these areas the West has developed beyond the East. As we often encounter them today, the ancient esoteric traditions are accidental conglomerations of useful techniques and outmoded cultural trappings. In such an atmosphere, a reduced form of meditation can be mass-merchandised.

And for many, their entire association with the techniques of meditation has been with the most rudimentary and minor form, that of a concentrative repetition, divorced from any cultural background, and divorced from other techniques that are organically associated with it. It is like learning how to spell, without ever learning how to read.

Continual concentration upon any object produces certain biological results. Among them is a loss of contact with the external world—which may be interpreted differently by a person merely amusing himself by staring at a crack in the wall, or by a person in a psychological experiment, or by one who performs these actions at the beginning of serious practice in esoteric tradition. One particular form of this concentrative meditation, known by its trademarked name as "Transcendental Meditation," is in fact the most elemental and least transcendent form of meditation of all. Indeed, Transcendental Meditation, quite popular in the United States and Western Europe, has offered many their first idea of what these traditions are about—unfortunately, too often in the form of a giggling, smiling guru and a highly developed program of scientific "validation." Descriptions of the efficacy of Transcendental Meditation are displayed in brochures and on posters stuck on laundromats and pizza parlors from Spokane to Boca Raton: "Improves levels of rest,

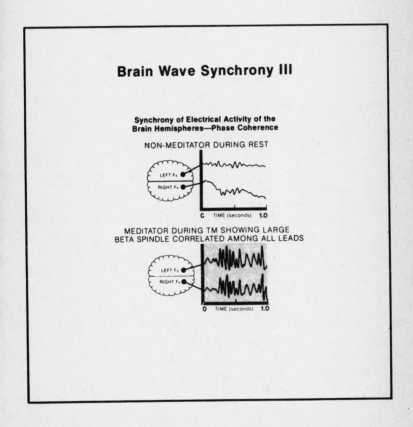

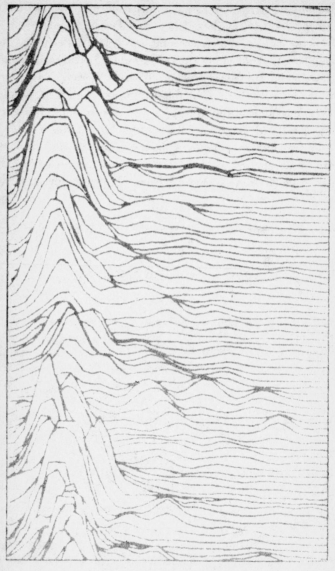

Computer-generated Fourier spectral analysis of electroencephalograph signals taken during Transcendental Meditation, showing a long period of pure, high amplitude, single-frequency theta waves.

aids natural changes in breath rate, cardiac output, relaxation, restful alertness, brain wave synchrony, faster reaction time, increased perceptual ability, learning ability, academic performance, productivity, job satisfaction, job performance, self-actualization, inner control, mental health, psychology," and so on. Indeed, it is claimed by the proselytizers of "TM" that it is the "answer to all your problems." Nowhere do we see reference to the major mental purpose of meditation; we are given only the reduction. Common to many of the franchised systems are these commercial claims to improve every aspect of human life. This is a mark of a cult system. Participants believe they have in their grasp a technique good for everyone at all times—not one that might have selective benefits and detriments.

In the case of TM, the bulk of its claimed scientific "validations" are usually marked "submitted for publication"—or are published by the movement's own Maharishi International University Press. TM is promoted as a synthesis of East and West— which means, presumably, that Western science is at last considered able to investigate practices of the East. If there *is* a synthesis here, it is an unfortunately comic one—the lack of scientific rigor in the East joined with the lack of spiritual advancement of the West. Such claims constitute a debasement of both science and meditation. Here, science is employed to document improvements in personality, or bodily changes, with no consideration given to whether such changes are in fact due to meditation, and what the significance of the change really is.

For instance, the mere report of an alteration in the electroencephalogram means almost nothing by itself. The EEG alone is quite an unstable measure, and rigorous controls must be maintained to ensure that it actually relates to significant brain activity. Recording an EEG might be compared to placing a heat sensor over a computer and attempting thereby to determine the computer's program. The innumerable brochures and posters which promote the TM movement often go beyond scientific evidence. "Increased synchrony" of the brain, for example, which connotes to those versed neither in meditation nor in brain research a measure of the mind's "increased harmony," that both hemispheres are working together, is often claimed as a result of TM. In truth, such "synchrony" (a finding largely unrepeated) derives from the fact that the brain may produce more alpha rhythm in times of quiescence, and thus the correlation of the two hemispheres of the brain is increased. Similarly, a time-displaced frequency (Fourier) analysis is sometimes displayed. The implication here is that the mind is "calm" during meditation, since the graphs have an appearance of regularity. This is merely the use of undigested technical vocabulary to impress the credulous. The pattern of an epileptic seizure might well look, to the uninitiated, as a coherent pattern on a frequency analysis. And thus with the relaxation measures, and the various additional studies. The fallacious and promotive scientism here seems to be: if any psychological or physiological measure alters during their practice of the concentrative "transcendental" meditation, then

a. it must be due, exclusively, to this wonderful practice; and

b. the change must be "good."

The studies continually barrage one with measures of increased Goodness and decreased Badness, during and after the practices.

Note how the process works. Herewith a proposed physiological experiment which will yield positive results, and which could be repeated (or, rather, performed for the first time) in any physiological laboratory in the world. I will also draw the same conclusions as do the TM merchandisers from their experiments (A and B). Suppose we assume that reading were not developed in our society. I might claim that reading "sacred" literature, such as the Bible, not only leads to increased Goodness, but that it *actually causes physiological changes*. Imagine the following experiment (C): physiological measures are taken on selected subjects before reading, while reading, and after

reading; eye movement is chosen for the physiological validation of our experiment.

We could naturally conclude that before reading, physiological activity was at a low level, but during reading it dra-
matically increased, and returned to baseline afterwards. If we
wanted to continue the research, we could undoubtedly record
alterations in Regional Cerebral Blood Flow (RCBF) to the left
hemisphere, changes in Galvanic Skin Resistance (GSR), etc.
However, our experiment would not explain how an arbitrary
measure, such as eye movement, relates to the supposed benefits
of reading, or whether, for instance, other types of reading
would show similar effects on the eye-movement measure.

Several points need to be raised about research attempting
to validate meditation. This kind of research tends to be promotive and exploitative; it uses science to sell a product. This promo-
tionalism is rather like drug-company television commercials that
show one product entering the bloodstream faster than others.
The essential question should be: what is the real effect of
meditation? Popular forms of meditation are, most likely, a
quite reduced and sanitized form of a more advanced exercise,
no more useful than repeating the words "Coca-Cola" or
"money" over and over for relaxation. This exercise is not at all
useless in itself, especially in cases of stress, but as it is packaged
it is quicksand to someone seeking extended knowledge.

The problems of promotive hucksterism are to be expected
when so few people are sufficiently acquainted with the intention, possibility, and range of esoteric traditions. Certainly,
relaxation of habitual thought patterns, and internal control, as
developed in esoteric tradition, can be of help to many people,
especially those prone to anxiety and worry. It may even enable
"normal" people to stabilize their health and achieve a more
flexible repertoire of thought strategies, as a prelude to involvement in esoteric traditions. However, the primary purpose of
meditation is not physiological. No one meditates to attain
"synchrony of electrical activity of the brain hemispheres" or

"a long period of pure, high-amplitude, single-frequency theta waves." Meditation is undertaken to increase one's capacity for experience and self-understanding.

The mental "emptiness" achieved by the concentrative forms of meditation is not a mere lapse in attention but an alteration in one's basic approach to the world, a glimpse of a potential consciousness. Other exercises, such as the "mindfulness" rituals in Zen, are intended to yield in the observer a notation of habitual sequential patterns of mental activity characteristic of the individual. There are a myriad of potential consciousness-alteration techniques. As our culture is opened up to the East,

IMAGINARY EXPERIMENT ON EFFECTS OF READING ON PHYSIOLOGICAL PROCESSES

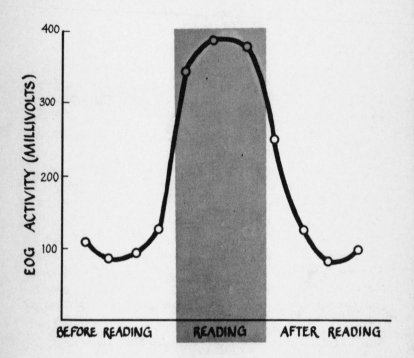

various immigrants have entered with techniques borrowed
piecemeal across cultures.

However, although there are many techniques available,
most people are not in a position to choose which technique
is most appropriate for them. There is, after all, no indigenous
cultural tradition to draw upon. "Experts" who have little experience of the unity and coherence of spiritual techniques offer
instant-weekend self-improvement courses which promote the
particular amalgam chosen by the expert himself. They often
involve a little meditation, a little indoctrination, a little scien-
tology, and a little "validation," with the audience softened up
(as in the best of brainwashing) by fatigue, fasting, and insults.
Such courses bear the same relationship to a consistent, spiritual
developed teaching as the techniques of a sex manual have to the
experience of love.*

The instant-enlightenment weekend approach can be produced by several means. One could duplicate the results by techniques as diverse as the proper use of jewelry, or by fasting, by
dancing to exhaustion, by sensory deprivation or overload, or
with drugs. Such an upset of ordinary activities and consciousness
yields a "first experience" that the world is different from what
one had thought. Yet, as a "first experience," we are likely to
misinterpret its significance, just as people often overvalue
their first sexual experience. We often find any real benefit to the
student plowed back into service to the organization.

If, for instance, you had never heard of an automobile, you
might be excited to be offered, for $50,000, a vehicle that actu-
ally ran on gasoline. Such a vehicle might be comprised of the
fenders of a 1921 Ford, the engine of a 1926 Hispano-Suiza, the
transmission of a contemporary Mercedes, seats from a Chevrolet
pickup truck, the rear body from an Austin. You might be further impressed by the sacrifices and the submission you and
many volunteers would need to keep such a vehicle on the road.

---

* I once received a form letter (with a computer address label) from one
West Coast instant guru that ended with "I love you."

If no one else of your acquaintance, however, had ever heard of an automobile, you might well become famous as the person "who gave it all up for the vehicle that could move itself." Yet even the most humble contemporary economy car would be an improvement.

The franchised weekends take just such an advantage of the gap in our education. Popular mysticism claims "converted" adherents for techniques which should be part of our basic education. Its enthusiasts take a partial aspect of esoteric tradition, such as an exercise meant for one community, and generalize it to everyone, and offer the same mass indoctrination or initiation to everyone. The initial "experience," then, is often channeled, not into the individual's personal development, but into the service of the system. Since the systems are synthetic and artificial amalgams, they must be kept going with much infusion of effort and activity. Thus, social gratification begins to substitute for the development of consciousness, with parties, mixers, investment clubs, phone solicitation, uniform dress, and jargon designed to create an elite in-group. Continual reminders are given to stragglers, by mass mailings, letters and phone calls, Christmas gifts, solicitations of service to the head of the organization, all consequence of the artificial nature of the system. The question is not only whether the constellation of techniques has any effect, but also whether in the long run the usefulness of the experience or the technique is outweighed by the benefits of the system itself, whether people seeking to develop themselves are ultimately exploited by those who confuse the container with the content.

II

The noncommercial, secretive, esoteric cults are unfortunately similar to the well-advertised consciousness systems. The degeneration of a true religious tradition in the West has left those high-minded "metaphysical people" prey to those who substitute an ancient fragmentary teaching for a unified whole. David Pendlebury describes the current situation:

> "Sobriety" and "intoxication" are of course not intended literally; nor are they merely flowery metaphors: these are technical terms denoting twin poles of human awareness, each in its own way indispensable to balanced development. A man has to see the true reality of his situation; he has to take a very sober look at himself. Equally, though, he needs a taste of another condition in which his latent possibilities are recognized. Taken on its own, either pole is sterile, developmentally speaking. There are plentiful examples all around us of such imbalances. Perhaps you too had a Calvinist great-uncle who died heartbroken, having succeeded in convincing himself, a. that "the grace of God" was essential, and b. that such "grace" had been withheld from him. Perhaps you, too, have friends whose Ouspensky-oriented understanding of Gurdjieff has left them eternally bewailing the (obvious) facts that "man is asleep," "man cannot remember himself," "man cannot do," etc. Or other friends who have chosen to "freak out," to "blow their minds"; and are astonished, in rare moments of lucidity, to find themselves inhabiting a "behavioural sink" or "terminal sewer." Or other friends, perhaps, who inform you in and out of season that: "I was hopelessly at sea, until (name and address supplied) showed me the answer."

Pendlebury mentions the Caucasian "mystic" George Gurdjieff, whose followers unfortunately have come to represent the fragmentation of much of contemporary esoteric studies. Although by many accounts Gurdjieff was a man who *personally* could awaken a sense of life and action in his associates, his work has become the captive of his most doctrinaire and severe followers, who seem to cherish their incompleteness and merely shout "I must wake up" while reading obsolete doctrines. A fragment of a coherent approach has become honored among those who look to each new teacher for the secret that will allow them to turn away from their morbid self-preoccupation and experience the wholeness of life.

This kind of esoteric school serves to promote the abnormality of those involved. Thus, the continuous search for "true teachers" of mysticism often leads enthusiasts to an examination and popularization of the past, of teachings inappropriate for our time and culture. Outmoded books on alchemy, ancient mysticism, commentaries on Gurdjieff and other mystics are all scoured by the devout in their hope of finding "the key" which will unite all. One of Gurdjieff's teachers describes this process to one who sought out the teachings of the East: "You are scrabbling about in the sands, looking for bits of mica to piece together to make a mirror, not realizing that the sand *itself* is capable of being transformed into the purest glass."

Here, then, is an essential distinction between the obscurantist esotericizers, who continually proclaim to "search the heavens" and the "depths of their souls" for isolated bits of knowledge, and a potentially viable contemporary spiritual teaching. Reductionism, or inflation, can exist on all levels, including the metaphysical. Merely writing in effulgent and self-denigratory terms about an outmoded cosmology is no more relevant to the real development of human knowledge than are psychiatric theorizing or the double-talk of commercial awareness-training groups. That the dead hand of a cold, sterile Metaphysical Inflationism should have touched the students of Gurdjieff—a man, for all his shortcomings, who always sought genuine development—is a great irony.

If there do exist so many difficulties in popularizing the fragmentary remains of esoteric tradition—a meditation technique that is sold for everybody, a man screaming for hours effectively brainwashing an audience, or a turgid "metaphysics" —then what might currently be useful in preparing the ground?

Most of the contemporary fragmentary systems suffer from

a confusion of the *essence* of mystical tradition with the original system itself. They often confuse the system with the knowledge, mixing up mistranslated ancient descriptions of "sight" and what can be "seen" with the technical details of an operation designed, say, to remove occlusions. A blind person accustomed to hearing inflated exaltations of the joys of sight may not be prepared when someone introduces technical procedures that are actually useful in an eye operation. "What are these cold hard things I touch?" he may exclaim of the surgical instruments. "What is their relationship to the grandeur of green grass, or to a sunset, of which I have heard so many wondrous descriptions?" Why many people of differing specializations may need to be involved in the task of surgery; why there is a need for antisepsis, for someone to have studied the physiology of the eye (or brain hemisphere, in the case of hemianopia), would entirely escape those who have become diverted from the attempt at *seeing* into a mere interest and expertise on "the dimensions of spiritual experience," "techniques of mysticism," "traditional approaches to the mind," or "the wisdom of the East." Such a person wishes for more availability of effulgent and high-minded descriptions of sight: the fragmentary substitute.

This is a continuous difficulty: the confusion of the vehicle with the objective, of the hard technical knowledge available in this area today with romantic descriptions of the universe, "spiritual experiences," "beings" of all orders, a "cosmic law." However, current literature, travel writings, and scientific facts all can serve a valid and reconstructive purpose: if properly presented, they can convey to the interested student the rudiments of "sight," and can aid in developing a more comprehensive awareness of himself and of life. This can occur even though the literature may not directly mention cosmology, God, mysticism, or any of the things most usually, romantically and traditionally, associated with mystical experience. Many of the most important books, then, do not appear in "metaphysical" collections, nor are they used by mystical societies. They may not contain one word of reference to this area, or be labeled "metaphysical." They are present but are "invisible" to the hemianopic, or to the blind slave of tradition, or to the devotee of the current cults.

Yakoub of Somnan, explaining the function of the literature that he used, said:

> Literature is the means by which things which have been taken out of the community, such as knowledge, can be returned.
>
> The similitude is as of a seed, which may be returned to the earth long after the plant from which it grew is dead, with perhaps no trace of it remaining.
>
> The learned may be millers of the grain-seed, but those whom we call the Wise are the cultivators of the crop.
>
> Take heed of this parable, for it contains the explanation of much irreconcilability of attitudes in the two classes of students.

8

A Spiritual
Psychology for
the Mainstream:
Contemporary
Sufism

To be a Sufi is to become what you can become and not to try to pursue what is, at the wrong stage, illusion.

It is to become aware of what is possible to you and not to think that you are aware of that of which you are heedless.

Sufism is the science of stilling what has to be stilled and alerting what can be alerted; not thinking that you can still or alert where you cannot, or that you need to do so when you do not need it.

—Sayed Imam Ali Shah

Between the reductionism of the Freudian or behavioristic sort on the one hand and the metaphysical inflation on the other, there does remain a useful area of pursuit of spiritual endeavors. However, it must be pursued at the proper level of its function, and not diverge into cosmology, tantrum Yoga, or outmoded theology. A scientist may unduly restrict himself to a single technique, or to what can be conventionally measured; a metaphysicizer to a romantic cosmic outpouring. Both may miss the mark, since any activity, from ordinary commerce to weather forecasting to cosmology, involves the understanding of simultaneous interactions. Thus, a consciousness needs to be developed which can encompass multiple levels of phenomena. A contemporary spiritual projection cannot demand either enslavement or a revival of guruism. Here, I attempt to provide a beginning commentary on a spiritual psychology relevant to contemporary life.

The High Knowledge

Anis was asked, "What is Sufism?"

He said, "Sufism is that which succeeds in bringing to man the High Knowledge."

"But if I apply the traditional methods handed down by the masters, is that not Sufism?"

"It is not Sufism if it does not perform its function for you. A cloak is no longer a cloak if it does not keep a man warm."

"So Sufism does change?"

"People change and needs change. So what was Sufism once is Sufism no more.

"Sufism," continued Anis, "is the external face of internal knowledge, known as High Knowledge. The inner factor does not change. The whole work, therefore, is the High Knowledge, plus capacity, which produces method. What you are pleased to call Sufism is merely the record of past method."

Generally speaking, the aim of a contemporary mysticism is to open another mode of knowledge to the practitioner. We speak of it as "High Knowledge," "Deep Understanding," or sometimes simply "Wisdom." "Wisdom" is a faculty that we normally associate with venerable old men and women who have seen patterns recur in life. The intent of a developed spiritual psychology is to provide a concentrated training in intuitive perception. These terms and techniques have a specific meaning within the discipline of Sufism, and refer to an experiential, not merely intellectual, understanding of many of the ultimate questions of philosophy and psychology.

The methods of contemporary Sufism are a means by which such understanding is brought about. The "knowledge" has at times been the province of philosophical, religious, esoteric, and occult systems. Many of the rituals and practices with which we are most familiar today are the remnants of those systems, diluted and reduced over time. Therefore, the first order of business is to distinguish past practices from current methodology. The "body of knowledge" that is Sufism has taken many forms, depending upon the culture and people who comprise it. It has existed within Hindu, Zoroastrian, Jewish, Christian, and nonreligious frameworks. It is, of course, best known in the West as a development of Classical Islam. Proficiency in Islamic studies is not, however, a requirement for the understanding of Sufism.

This diversity of form and technique is one reason for the "invisibility" of Sufism. Since they have existed across cultures and eras, Sufis are not so easily identifiable as disciples of more technique-centered, high-profile forms of metaphysics. Obviously, involvement in Sufism takes a different form for each person and for each culture, since its activity exists at a more comprehensive level than does the individual.

Within Islam itself, Sufism has been considered a "flower"— the highest development of Islamic preachings. With a current revival of interest in Sufism, sparked largely by the writings of Idries Shah, many students have extended their interest to the classical, theological versions of Sufism, which are a product of the Middle East. But some of this interest is archaeological and anthropological as well as spiritual: these two separate kinds of interest must be distinguished at the outset. The belief that Sufism must be Islamic is a mere Middle Eastern ethnocentrism, the confusion of yeast itself with one particular loaf of bread.

The Tale of the Sands

A stream, from its source in far-off mountains, passing through every kind and description of countryside, at last reached the sands of the desert. Just as it had crossed every other barrier, the stream tried to cross this one, but it found that as fast as it ran into the sand, its waters disappeared.

It was convinced, however, that its destiny was to cross this desert, and yet there was no way. Now a hidden voice, coming from the desert itself, whispered: "The wind crosses the desert, and so can the stream."

The stream objected that it was dashing itself against the sand, and only getting absorbed: that the wind could fly and this was why it could cross a desert.

"By hurtling in your own accustomed way you cannot get across. You will either disappear or become a marsh. You must allow the wind to carry you over to your destination."

But how could this happen?

"By allowing yourself to be absorbed in the wind."

This idea was not acceptable to the stream. After all, it had never been absorbed before. It did not want to lose its individuality. And, once having lost it, how was one to know that it could ever be regained?

"The wind," said the sand, "performs this function. It takes up water, carries it over the desert, and then lets it fall again. Falling as rain, the water again becomes a river."

"How can I know that is true?"

"It is so, and if you do not believe it, you cannot become more than a quagmire, and even that could take many, many years; and it certainly is not the same as a stream."

"But can I not remain the same stream that I am today?"

"You cannot in either case remain so," the whisper said. "Your essential part is carried away and forms a stream again. You are called what you are even today because you do not know which part of you is the essential one."

When he heard this, certain echoes began to arise in the

thoughts of the stream. Dimly, he remembered a state in which he—or some part of him, was it?—had been held in the arms of a wind. He also remembered—or did he?—that this was the real thing, not necessarily the obvious thing to do.

And the stream raised his vapour into the welcoming arms of the wind, which gently and easily bore it upwards and along, letting it fall softly as soon as they reached the roof of a mountain, many, many miles away. And because he had had his doubts, the stream was able to remember and record more strongly in his mind the details of the experience. He reflected, "Yes, now I have learned my true identity."

The stream was learning. But the sands whispered: "We know, because we see it happen day after day: and because we, the sands, extend from the riverside all the way to the mountain."

And that is why it is said that the way in which the Stream of Life is to continue on its journey is written in the Sands.

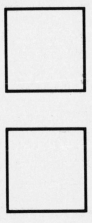

Show a man too many camel's bones, or show them to him too often, and he will not be able to recognize a camel when he comes across a live one.

—Miraza Ahsan of Tabriz

Another, and equally important, reason for the lack of a fixed system in any contemporary form of mysticism is that the primary questions that might lead one to mysticism, such as "What is the meaning of life?" and "What is the nature of man?" cannot, as we have seen, be answered in any systematic manner. An adequate treatment of these questions lies within the realm of personal experiential knowledge, in the life situations of individuals. To pose these questions in purely academic terms is inappropriate, an unfortunate mixture of levels of analysis, and often results in a mere incomprehensible doctrine such as the "universe and Man" or "the Great Cosmic Design." That many bizarre and absurd notions are continually associated with spirituality does not mean, as the positivists would have it, that these important questions should not be asked. It is, rather, a matter of the appropriateness of the response and the differing mode of the question.

There is no fixed system in mystic studies, no unchanging dogma which one *must* follow. If Sufism is often said to be "too sublime to have a history," this is, in part, the reason. As Sufism has developed throughout different cultural eras, it has become impervious to literalism. If it were possible to attain a relevant spirituality—"to open one's eyes," or to develop an extended consciousness—in a systematic manner, that system would have been written long ago. This has not been possible partly because people have possessed differing strengths and weaknesses in different cultures. The appropriate development or concentration for one civilization may be useless or even harmful for another. Conditions of life change, understandings progress and regress, and the "ground" in which Sufism grows changes. Since Sufism is thus an "organic" process, it too becomes different in each age and tradition. For instance, ideas and practices which may have been of great interest within a rural economy two hundred years ago are no longer of much import. The particular system must always be considered temporary. All "Sufis" do not always do the same things, and are not always members of the same organizations or "in-groups." They are not necessarily alike, or even obviously associated.

Most Sufi writers maintain, then, that any "system" (or even specific methodologies) or any school of Sufism must be distinguished from the "knowledge" of Sufism at the outset of study. Too often, adherents of one particular system (which may originally have been of great use) tend to identify it with the "only way," the only knowledge. This is the first stage in the calcifying of a spiritual school. The original system becomes venerated and fixed, with followers of the original leader reverting to scriptural discussion of what fixed principles should be applied in every case. Then a once-useful enterprise begins to degenerate and becomes like a fossil: fixed, frozen at one historical moment. This is the same process we find in contemporary life: a government office takes over an original program, and then the program is subverted to prolong and perpetuate its own bureaucracy. Partly for these reasons, Sufis are often sent to study different traditions, in order to broaden the overall range of information available in one culture, to distinguish the "system" from the "knowledge" and the knowledge from its cultural environment.

Once the interested student is prepared, he can consider many diverse approaches to knowledge, and can learn to understand their workings and relevance to him, yet remain inoculated against the exclusive claims of cults and partial, piecemeal systems.

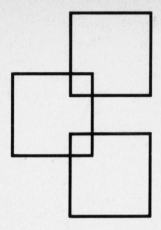

Just as the principles of Sufism are not immediately reducible to a frozen, formal system, neither, unfortunately, is "progress" in the development of a complete consciousness. The fixed system and the concept of "spiritual progress" are, however, associated. Currently there are many people who pursue "enlightenment," who create a market for the conceptions of discrete "levels of spiritual development" in metaphysical inflationist journals and books. These levels are often studied carefully by people looking for the fast answer (people anxious to identify their own very first moments of an extended consciousness and to have others find out about their developments as soon as possible). There is in Sufism, however, little place or consideration given such obsessive seekers, no matter how attractive a discipline Sufism may be to such people. The difficulty is that obsessional thought in *any* discipline, spiritual or otherwise, can consume the seeker. An untoward "spiritual progress" can become a substitute for social responsibility or for one's job, and a detriment in personal situations.

This type of thought on the nature of a developed esoteric knowledge (and it is quite common) is at once the product of our contemporary miseducation and of personal psychological panic or derangement, merely overlaid on the process of mysticism. It should be understood that many individuals who seek an instant form of relief from their personal incompetence, guilt, or inability to "relate," in any culturally approved manner, to other people are not likely to find an escapist haven for themselves in any real contemporary mysticism. Sufism, for instance, is not a form of mushed-under psychotherapy promising instant relief, nor a substitute for ordinary on-the-job training. It should neither be considered an *extension* of the world of psychotherapy, nor self-preoccupation, nor fast-food for thought. The current cultural difficulty is that many people who are trained to believe that they need help in their personal lives mistakenly assume that "higher studies" will give them what they seek. (Whether such help is really needed and whether there is any useful cultural mechanism for dealing with such needs is touched on in the chapter on psychiatroid mentation.) Yet probably worse than the confusion in the public is that of the practitioners of therapy themselves, who often offer a warmed-over mash of misinterpreted religion, reduced or inflated, and an attempt at "good feeling" or "good vibes" to their often unwary clients.

One should, of course, not hold that personal problems never do exist. These difficulties, whether in the realm of interpersonal relations, illiteracy, poor nutrition, or social and cultural difficulties, must be met and tolerably answered *before* one's involvement in esoteric studies begins. Otherwise, this study can become reduced to an appendage to, and magnifier of, a person's difficulty. Once personal problems are met, the irrational desire for visible "progress" and for the comfort of a secure system of mysticism may be lessened.

The miseducation component still remains. We must appreciate that individuals differ and that the principles of a mystical teaching are different for different societies. Thus, the "steps on the path" or an "entry into another world" will not be the same for everyone. As we have considered, the discussion of "another world" is a device, a constructive metaphor for another order of thought, consciousness, and being. It is often romanticized, inflated, and made external to the person, often to the point of unattainability. Yet all people are not alike, and what is opportunity at one occasion for one person may be a difficulty for another. The common error is "looking to the heavens" for a sign or for a comforting indication of progress when opportunities for enlightenment may abound in the life of the person. Here are two stories on the subject, both from *Tales of the Dervishes*.

The Man with the Inexplicable Life

There was once a man named Mojud. He lived in a town where he had obtained a post as a small official, and it seemed likely that he would end his days as Inspector of Weights and Measures.

One day when he was walking through the gardens of an ancient building near his home Khidr, the mysterious Guide of the Sufis, appeared to him, dressed in shimmering green. Khidr said: "Man of bright prospects! Leave your work and meet me at the riverside in three days' time." Then he disappeared.

Mojud went to his superior in trepidation and said that he had to leave. Everyone in the town soon heard of this and they said: "Poor Mojud! He has gone mad!" But, as there were many candidates for his job, they soon forgot him.

On the appointed day, Mojud met Khidr, who said to him, "Tear your clothes and throw yourself into the stream. Perhaps someone will save you."

Mojud did so, even though he wondered if he were mad.

Since he could swim, he did not drown, but drifted a long way before a fisherman hauled him into his boat, saying "Foolish man! The current is strong. What are you trying to do?"

Mojud said: "I do not really know."

"You are mad," said the fisherman, "but I will take

you into my reed-hut by the river yonder, and we shall see what can be done for you."

When he discovered that Mojud was well-spoken, he learned from him how to read and write. In exchange, Mojud was given food and helped the fisherman with his work. After a few months, Khidr again appeared, this time at the foot of Mojud's bed, and said: "Get up now and leave this fisherman. You will be provided for."

Mojud immediately quit the hut, dressed as a fisherman, and wandered about until he came to a highway. As dawn was breaking he saw a farmer on a donkey on his way to market. "Do you seek work?" asked the farmer. "Because I need a man to help me to bring back some purchases."

Mojud followed him. He worked for the farmer for nearly two years, by which time he had learned a great deal about agriculture but little else.

One afternoon when he was baling wool, Khidr appeared to him and said: "Leave that work, walk to the city of Mosul, and use your savings to become a skin merchant."

Mojud obeyed.

In Mosul he became known as a skin merchant, never seeing Khidr while he plied his trade for three years. He had saved quite a large sum of money, and was thinking of buying a house, when Khidr appeared and said: "Give me your money, walk out of this town as far as distant Samarkand, and work for a grocer there." Mojud did so.

Presently he began to show undoubted signs of illumination. He healed the sick, served his fellow men in the shop and during his spare time, and his knowledge of the mysteries became deeper and deeper.

Clerics, philosophers and others visited him and asked: "Under whom did you study?"

"It is difficult to say," said Mojud.

His disciples asked: "How did you start your career?"

He said: "As a small official."

"And you gave it up to devote yourself to self-mortification?"

"No, I just gave it up."

They did not understand him.

People approached him to write the story of his life.

"What have you been in your life?" they asked.

"I jumped into a river, became a fisherman, then walked out of his reed-hut in the middle of one night. After that, I became a farmhand. While I was baling wool, I changed and went to Mosul, where I became a skin merchant. I saved some money there, but gave it away. Then I walked to Samarkand where I worked for a grocer. And this is where I am now."

"But this inexplicable behavior throws no light upon your strange gifts and wonderful examples," said the biographers.

"That is so," said Mojud.

So the biographers constructed for Mojud a wonderful and exciting history; because all saints must have their story, and the story must be in accordance with the appetite of the listener, not with the realities of the life.

And nobody is allowed to speak of Khidr directly. That is why this story is not true. It is a representation of a life. This is the real life of one of the greatest Sufis.

The Initiation of Malik Dinar

After many years' study of philosophical subjects, Malik Dinar felt that the time had come to travel in search of knowledge. "I will go," he said to himself, "seeking the Hidden Teacher, who is also said to be within my uttermost self."

Walking out of his house with only a few dates for provision, he came presently upon a dervish plodding along the dusty road. He fell into step alongside him, in silence for a time.

Finally the dervish spoke. "Who are you and where are you going?"

"I am Dinar, and I have started to journey in search of the Hidden Teacher."

"I am El-Malik El-Fatih, and I will walk with you," said the dervish.

"Can you help me to find the Teacher?" asked Dinar.

"Can I help you, can you help me?" asked Fatih, in the irritating manner of dervishes everywhere. "The hidden teacher, so they say, is in a man's self. How he finds him depends upon what use he makes of experience. This is something only partly conveyed by a companion."

Presently they came to a tree, which was creaking and swaying. The dervish stopped. "The tree is saying," he said after a moment, " 'Something is hurting me, stop awhile and take it out of my side so that I may find repose.' "

"I am in too much of a hurry," replied Dinar. "And how can a tree talk, anyway?" They went on their way.

After a few miles, the dervish said, "When we were near the tree I thought that I smelt honey. Perhaps it was a wild-bees' hive which had been built in its hole."

"If that is true," said Dinar, "let us hurry back, so that we may collect the honey, which we could eat, and sell some for the journey."

"As you wish," said the dervish.

When they arrived back at the tree, however, they saw some other travellers collecting an enormous quantity of honey. "What luck we have had!" these men said. "This is enough honey to feed a city. We poor pilgrims can now become merchants: our future is assured."

Dinar and Fatih went on their way.

Presently they came to a mountain on whose slopes they heard a humming. The dervish put his ear to the ground. Then he said: "Below us there are millions of ants, building a colony. This humming is a concerted plea for help. In ant-language it says: 'Help us, help us. We are excavating, but have come across strange rocks which bar our progress. Help dig them away.' Should we stop and help, or do you want to hasten ahead?"

"Ants and rocks are not our business, brother," said Dinar, "because I, for one, am seeking my Teacher."

"Very well, brother," said the dervish. "Yet they do say that all things are connected, and this may have a certain connection with us."

Dinar took no notice of the older man's mumblings, and so they went their way.

The pair stopped for the night, and Dinar found that he had lost his knife. "I must have dropped it near the ant-hill," he said. Next morning they retraced their way.

When they arrived back at the ant-hill, they could find no sign of Dinar's knife. Instead they saw a group of people, covered in mud, resting beside a pile of gold coins. "These," said the people, "are a hidden hoard which we have just dug up. We were on the road when a frail old dervish called to us: 'Dig at this spot and you will find that which is rocks to some but gold to others.'"

Dinar cursed his luck. "If we had only stopped," he said, "you and I would both have been rich last night, O Dervish." The other party said: "This dervish with you, stranger, looks strangely like the one whom we saw last night."

"All dervishes look very much alike," said Fatih. And they went their respective ways.

Dinar and Fatih continued their travels, and some days later they came to a beautiful river-bank. The dervish stopped and as they sat waiting for the ferry a fish rose several times to the surface and mouthed at them.

"This fish," said the dervish, "is sending us a message. It says: 'I have swallowed a stone. Catch me and give me a certain herb to eat. Then I will be able to bring it up, and will thus find relief. Travellers, have mercy!'"

At that moment the ferry-boat appeared and Dinar, impatient to get ahead, pushed the dervish into it. The boatman was grateful for the copper which they were able to give him, and Fatih and Dinar slept well that night on the opposite bank, where a teahouse for travellers had been placed by a charitable soul.

In the morning they were sipping their tea when the ferryman appeared. Last night had been his most fortunate one, he said; the pilgrims had brought him luck. He kissed the hands of the venerable dervish, to take his blessing. "You deserve it all, my son," said Fatih.

The ferryman was now rich: and this was how it happened. He was about to go home at his usual time, but he had seen the pair on the opposite bank, and resolved to make one more trip, although they looked poor, for the "baraka," the blessing of helping the traveller. When he was about to put away his boat, he saw the fish, which had thrown itself on the bank. It was apparently trying to swallow a piece of plant. The fisherman put the plant into its mouth. The fish threw up a stone and flopped back into the water. The stone was a huge and flawless diamond of incalculable value and brilliance.

"You are a devil!" shouted the infuriated Dinar to the dervish Fatih. "You knew about all three treasures by means of some hidden perception, yet you did not tell me at the time. Is *that* true companionship? Formerly, my ill-luck was strong enough: but without you I would not even have known of the possibilities hidden in trees, ant-hills and fish—of all things!"

No sooner had he said these words than he felt as though a mighty wind were sweeping through his very soul. And then he knew that the very reverse of what he had said was the truth.

The dervish, whose name means the Victorious King, touched Dinar lightly on the shoulder, and smiled. "Now brother, you will find that you can learn by experience. I am he who is at the command of the Hidden Teacher."

When Dinar dared to look up, he saw his Teacher walking down the road with a small band of travellers, who were arguing about the perils of the journey ahead of them.

Today the name Malik Dinar is numbered among the foremost of the dervishes, companion and exemplar, the Man Who Arrived.

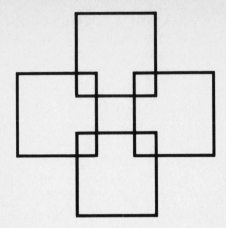

Sufism is not formal, canonical knowledge. Academic disciplines such as psychology, mathematics, and physics strive for "objectivity" and impersonal knowledge. Sufism depends on people, on experience. It is a way of looking at things—a way in which qualities are "caught" rather than formally taught.

Many have felt that Western science and education leave "something" out, yet they have little idea what it is or where to look for it. Gurus of every persuasion cater to this dissatisfaction. It is the appeal of substituting one set of inadequate rules for another, of searching for someone to *tell us* how to behave, how to live. Sufism excels in dealing with these questions, emphasizing again and again that spirituality is not social organization, not personality theory, not metaphysics. The Sufi current has existed for thousands of years in many cultures, within Hindu, Christian, Jewish, and other religious and nonreligious frameworks.

Perhaps the most distinguishing feature of Sufism is that it is truly contemporary. None of us is about to discard the very real advances of Western culture to become imitation twelfth-century Indians or Genuine Replicas of thirteenth-century Zen monks. Nor are many about to accept the "get-rich-quick" mysticism of the Sunday supplements. ("What's your sign, trait, type?") Absurd and often bizarre ideas have caused many sensible people to discount mystical teachings as a whole. When electricity was first introduced, all kinds of stories were told about it. Some thought the new invention would rob them of individuality, others that they would be immediately transported to paradise. Others ignored it. So too with an extended knowledge of psychology.

Since Sufism is not formal knowledge, one cannot write it out as one would an equation. Some presentations seem paradoxical. Sufism is not academic psychology as we know it, not Oriental studies, not history, not religion, not anthropology, not philosophy, not physics, not literature, not educational theory. But Sufis have contributed to all these areas.

Let me try another way of looking at the impact of a contemporary mysticism, a mysticism designed for the mainstream of our society. Western thinkers tend to specialize and compartmentalize themselves in ordinary attempts at knowledge-seeking. University departments, for example, often ignore the non-academic public and even valuable research evidence from other departments. Anthropologists often know little of history, physicists little of Oriental studies. Different disciplines are often considered independent probes sent into the unknown, seemingly in different directions. This can be described in a diagram:

In spite of this apparently increasing specialization and divergence, the ultimate questions of each discipline are closely related. "What is the nature of physical reality?" is much the same question as "What is the nature of life?" or "What is the nature of the mind?" Instead of being mutually exclusive, all these questions may be of a piece. The search for education, for religion, for scientific knowledge, may all converge at a point. We can align these probes in a different manner:

At the center of all human specializations lies *one thing*, contend the Sufis. The eight-pointed star is one of its symbols.

Three travelers who had one coin among them were arguing: "I want something sweet to eat," said one. "I want several sweet things to eat," said the second. "I want something thirst-quenching," said the third. A fourth man took their coin and bought grapes, which satisfied them all.

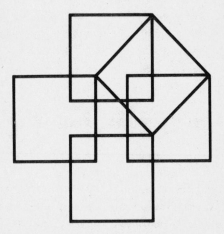

If much of the foregoing has dealt with what Sufism as an example of a contemporary "mysticism" is *not*, I hope that the reader will appreciate the need to clear away common misconceptions. There are, of course, expositions of Sufism which are readily available. Idries Shah has published more than a thousand "teaching tales" in English, as well as in other Western languages. These tales are not designed to inculcate moralisms or to be learned as rote facts, but to provide the means of communication of this consistent teaching. The earliest Sufi tale to bear the stamp of a constructed artifact designed to point to a form of reality normally imperceptible to man is found in the Koran. It is the tale of Khidr and Moses, reproduced by Shah in *Tales of the Dervishes.*

Although all these tales were originally intended by the dervish storytellers from the Middle East as "teaching stories," they have little in common with the parable or didactic story of most Western cultures. Instead of convincing the reader that a certain type of thought or action is good, these teaching stories illustrate patterns of human behavior, and lessons in intuitive wisdom, which could not be put in any other way. They guide the reader along unfamiliar philosophic paths. Some are meant to familiarize the reader with the unusual; and some are intended to shock—as a fresh stimulus to the mind to upset its normal patterns of thought. They constitute an education for both modes of knowledge at the same time.

In the stories, many of which contain sayings and doings of wise men and fools, we often find the sage playing the part of the ordinary man, demonstrating some course of action or train of thought which he is attempting to criticize. Other stories are open-minded—they provide no automatic solution, but rely on the reader to find his own interpretations.

Until 1964 this function of the "story of inner meaning" was all but completely unknown to most Western thinkers. Jalaluddin Rumi (in his *Masnavi-I-Maanavi* and *Fihi Ma Fihi*) employed some tales of this type quite extensively, yet, oddly, until Shah's *The Sufis* explained the special application of tales among the Sufis, many scholars regarded Rumi as a storyteller in the folklore and parable tradition, and some were even embarrassed by the Master's apparent fondness for mere jokes, anecdotes, and folk tales.

The literary and entertainment quality of these stories is in their "Moses' basket" aspect—their key to continued use and survival lies in their lack of dependence on specific cultural mores. But their aim, as Shah points out, is to "connect with a part of the individual which cannot be reached by any other convention, [and to] establish in him or in her a means of communication with a non-verbalized truth beyond the customary limitations of our familiar dimensions."

How and What to Understand

This interchange between the Sufi mystic Simab and a nobleman named Mulakab is preserved in oral transmission as a dialogue often staged by wandering dervishes:

Mulakab: "Tell me something of your philosophy, so that I may understand."

Simab: "You cannot understand unless you have experienced."

Mulakab: "I do not have to understand a cake to know whether it is bad."

Simab: "If you are looking at a good fish and you think that it is a bad cake, you need to understand less, and to understand it better, more than you need anything else."

Mulakab: "Then why do you not abandon books and lectures, if experience is the necessity?"

Simab: "Because 'the outward is the conductor to the inward.' Books will teach you something of the outward aspects of the inward, and so will lectures. Without them, you would make no progress."

Mulakab: "But why should we not be able to do without books?"

Simab: "For the same reason that you cannot think without words. You have been reared on books, your mind is so altered by books and lectures, by hearing and speaking, that the inward can only speak to you through the outward, whatever you pretend you can perceive."

Mulakab: "Does this apply to everyone?"

Simab: "It applies to whom it applies. It applies above all to those who think it does not apply to them!"

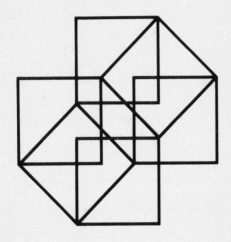

The Sage said:

"Fate continues. But on no account abandon your own intentions.

"For if your plans accord with the supreme will, you will attain a plenitude of fulfillment for your heart."

—Anwar-i-Suhaili

Many people, familiar only with degenerated religious and mystical groups, have difficulty understanding the ideas of "submission" and "alignment." The word "submission" often conjures up a grotesque image of a person yielding his attainments and "humbly" serving another. Or, perhaps, the selling of one's possessions as a total renunciation of the products of contemporary life. These misunderstandings are remnants of previous or distant "systems" which have so degenerated that the essence of their original concept is forgotten. Often the misunderstandings are sustained by people who are interested in keeping themselves from any real contact with this study, or by those who confuse Sufism and other systems with some kind of therapy.

The idea of submission, in contemporary terms, is related to the understanding that our conventional sources of education have not yielded answers to the basic questions of life, and that therefore we must turn to those who specialize in such matters, whose knowledge is superior in this area to ours. There is no mortification of a person who submits to superior knowledge in this manner. There is, however, the need for a clear distinction between what *should* be surrendered and what need not be. Bahaudin Naqshband, a Sufi teacher, related that he was at one time quite ready "to yield far more far-reaching" parts of himself than necessary, but was not prepared to yield the *minor* ones which were the barriers to his understanding.•

There is, for example, no need to give up meat, or reading, or logical analysis, or even normal social endeavors. There is no celibacy in Sufism, no adherence to a "leader." To shift the example, consider a parallel: What sort of surgeon would demand such behavior? He would not ask that a patient prostrate himself in order to obtain his specialized service, even though he may be the only one specially trained to aid in a life-threatening situation. One does not forever owe one's life to a surgeon after an operation, though it may indeed have saved one's life or given him vision. We would consider such behavior obviously inappropriate submission, yet one who knew little of medicine might not. Inappropriate also is the relinquishing of skills and competence in other areas, such as business or science, since these attributes are separate from the events in question. It is an unfortunate accident of our times that the area of metaphysics is now littered with submissive and "humble" occultists and others who neurotically feel that their intellectual, emotional, and family development must be discarded. They confuse "piety" and "humble" behavior with "humility." No doctor would put up with this kind of nonsense. Neither will a Sufi.

The "submission" that the doctor *does* demand, however, is the agreement to follow his regime of treatment and to employ the materials provided in the manner prescribed. At some moment in many ordinary endeavors, we place ourselves in the hands of others—when we learn to swim, when we have a suit made, when we learn a foreign language, when we obtain treatment for a health problem. Spiritual studies are no different.

There is no requirement to divest oneself of autonomy, identity, or competence, as some currently popular forms of spirituality require. A proper approach is to learn what is to be put into abeyance, to "wake up" in order that one's proper role may be assumed. This "alignment" is not a submission of identity, a smoothing out of "rough edges" or some sort of psychiatroid-inspired personality change. Here is a tale in which the Sufi does not try to divest his student of his identity, no matter how negative the student's strongest characteristic might appear.

The Man Who Was Easily Angered

A man who was very easily angered realized after many years that all his life he had been in difficulties because of this tendency.

One day he heard of a dervish deep of knowledge, whom he went to see, asking for advice.

The dervish said: "Go to such-and-such a crossroads. There you will find a withered tree. Stand under it and offer water to every traveller who passes that place."

The man did as he was told. Many days passed, and he became well known as one who was following a certain discipline of guidance and self-control under the instructions of a man of real knowledge.

One day a man in a hurry turned his head away when he was offered the water, and went on walking along the road.

The man who was easily angered called out to him several times: "Come, return my salutation! Have some of this water, which I provide for all travellers!"

But there was no reply.

Overcome by this behavior, the first man forgot his discipline completely. He reached for his gun, which was hooked in the withered tree, took aim at the heedless travel-ler and fired. The man fell dead.

At the very moment that the bullet entered his body, the withered tree, as if by a miracle, burst joyfully into blossom.

The man who had been killed was a murderer, on his way to commit the worst crime of a long career.

There are, you see, two kinds of advisers. The first kind is the one who tells what should be done according to certain fixed principles, repeated mechanically. The other kind is the Man of Knowledge. Those who meet the Man of Knowledge will ask him for moralistic advice, and will treat him as a moralist. But what he serves is Truth, not pious hopes.

In our conventional way of thinking, there is scarcely a trait worse than anger, or a crime worse than murder. The story is designed to shock by directly employing such tendencies and ac-tions since they illustrate the difference between conventional ideas of submission and "improvement" and the Sufi conception of alignment.

The Sufi does not attempt to "cure" the man of his difficulty. Rather, he attempts to align the man's dominant characteristics in a more comprehensive perception of the effects of action, and places him in a spot in which the "difficulty" can be of use.*

Within Sufism, there is no adulation of a remote Final Mystic Experience, a detached "higher consciousness," or the retired life of the ascetic on a mountaintop. Such experience has

---

* It may also be of some use here to consider the Sufi teacher, the man, the withered tree, and other elements in the story as aspects of a single personality.

been considered the end point, or pinnacle, of many religious and philosophical systems. However true this may be in systems which have persevered too long, it is not the case within contemporary Sufism. If one "wakes up" and remains in bed, then what is the use of awakening? How would the awakener differ from those also in bed, but asleep? For the Sufi, the "return to the world" is the return to and alignment with active life as it is lived, which distinguishes the full development of man.

Appetite

Firoz was asked: "The books and the very presence of a man of wisdom increase the appetite for learning in the public, and also in those who wish to understand the real meaning of man. Is it not harmful to excite the anticipation of those who may not be able to profit from the Teaching, and who are incapable of recognizing its beauty, meaning, and significance?"

He said, "Water will attract the greedy man, but that is no argument against water. There are greedy men who are excited at the sight of apricots. If they try to steal them, they may be punished. If their greed causes them to gobble them so that their stomachs cannot sustain the load, they become sick. The owner of the orchard does not become sick."

The questioner continued, "But in the interests of the thirsty man, could the water not be given to him in small amounts, so that he does himself no harm?"

Firoz said, "Sometimes there is a kindly person present who sees a crazed thirsty one, and he prevents him from killing himself through drinking too much. At other times, as you well know, the thirsty man comes across a well, and there is nobody there to prevent him from destroying himself. Even if there were a well-meaning bystander to say 'Be careful!', the man erazed with thirst would thrust him aside and believe him to be his enemy."

The questioner asked, "Is there no way in which a person may be safeguarded against these perils?"

Firoz told him, "If you can find anything in this life which is without any danger of abuse and lacks risk for the stupid, tell me, and I shall myself spend all my time concentrating upon that thing. In the meantime learn, before it may be too late, that the guide exists because the path is rough. If you, so to speak, want to be able to breathe in without breathing out, or to waken up without facing the day—you are no Seeker, but a mere trumpery dilettante, and a hypocrite at that, for to call oneself something which one is not is contrary to the dignity of the people of dedication and straightforwardness."

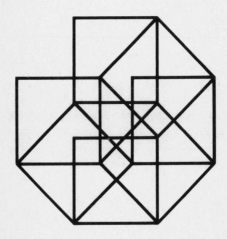

There is no profession of endeavor which has any claim to being closer to a more complete consciousness than any other. As we have described earlier, the study of consciousness is at the center of conventional thought in many areas, and carries worth for people of different countries, classes, and specializations. Here follow two stories on the relation of "mystic" to ordinary activities.

Meatballs

Awad Afifi was asked, "Which kinds of worldly happening can conduce towards the understanding of the Sufi Way?"

He said, "I shall give you an illustration when it is possible."

Some time later, Awad and some of his group were on a visit to a garden outside their city.

A number of rough mountaineer nomads were encamped by the wayside. Awad stopped and bought a small piece of roast meat from one nomad, who had set up a Kebab stall there.

As he raised the meat to his lips, the stall-keeper uttered a cry and fell to the ground in a strange state. Then he stood up, took Awad's hand and kissed it.

Awad said, "Let us be on our way." Accompanied by the roast-meat man, all proceeded along the highroad.

This nomad's name was Koftapaz (meatball-cook), and he was soon revealed as one whose *baraka*, spiritual power, gave meaning and effect to the spiritual exercises of the whole School.

Awad called his followers together and said, "I have been asked which kind of worldly happening can conduce towards the understanding of the Sufi Way.

"Let those who were present at the meeting with Koftapaz tell those who were not there, and then let Koftapaz himself give the explanation, for he is now my appointed Deputy."

When all had been informed about the encounter on the way to the garden, Sheikh Koftapaz stood up and said, "O people upon whom the shadow of the beneficent bird Simurgh has rested! Know that all my life I have been a maker of meatballs.

"Therefore it was easy for me to know the Master by the way in which he raised a morsel to his lips—for I had seen the inwardness of every other kind of mortal by his outwardness; and if you are totally accomplished in your own work, you may recognize your Imam (leader) by his relationship with your work."

Duty

A certain Sufi was asked, "People come for companionship, discourses and teaching. Yet you plunge them into activity. Why is this?"

He said, "Though they—and you—may believe that they come for enlightenment, they mainly desire engagement in something. I give them engagement as a means of learning.

"Those who become totally engaged are they who sought only engagement, and who could not profit by self-observation of themselves so uselessly engaged. It is, therefore, not the deep respecters of activity who become illuminated."

The questioner said, "Who, then, is it who does become illuminated?"

The Sufi replied, "The illuminated are those who perform duties adequately, realizing that there is something beyond."

"But how is that 'something beyond' to be reached?"

"It is always reached by those who perform adequately. They need no further instruction. If you were doing your duty adequately, and were neither neglectful nor fanatically attached to it, you would not have had to ask the question."

And yet can the grand "metaphysical" problems, which are written of at such length, be subject to such an elegantly simple formulation? One cannot answer this kind of question directly. As an illustrative example, however, one can note that the simplest of elements, if "aligned" correctly, can produce a whole of great interest and complexity, functioning simultaneously on several levels. Such a complex entity is one to which many would attribute very grand, perhaps inflated and complex origins. But, to take an example, the final illustration in the series appearing throughout this chapter is comprised simply of eight squares, set at 45-degree angles to one another, yet upon study its multiple organization is apparent.

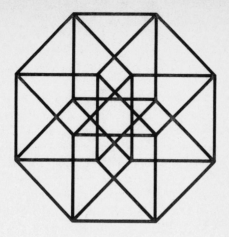

Contrary to Expectation

A wise man, the wonder of his age, taught his disciples from a seemingly inexhaustible store of wisdom.

He attributed all his knowledge to a thick tome which was kept in a place of honour in his room.

The sage would allow nobody to open the volume.

When he died, those who had surrounded him, regarding themselves as his heirs, ran to open the book, anxious to possess what it contained.

They were surprised, confused and disappointed when they found that there was writing on only one page.

They became even more bewildered, and then annoyed, when they tried to penetrate the meaning of the phrase which met their eyes.

It was: "When you realise the difference between the container and the content, you will have knowledge."

Notes

The chapter-opening designs are taken from J. Bourgoin, *Arabic Geometrical Pattern and Design*, a Dover, New York, reprint (1973) of an 1879 publication, *Les Elements de l'Art Arabe: le Trait des Entrelacs*. I would like to thank Dover for allowing so many illustrations to be reprinted.

1. The Container and the Content

The most useful single edition of the works of Jallaludin Rumi is the E. H. Whinfield translation and abridgement, *Teachings of Rumi*, (Dutton, New York, 1975).

In addition, A. J. Arberry has provided many excerpts from Rumi's work in his *Tales of the Masnavi* (George Allen & Unwin, London, 1961) and *More Tales of the Masnavi* (1963).

Jacob Bronowski's *The Ascent of Man* (Little, Brown, Boston, 1973) is often brilliant and well-illustrated on the rise of contemporary science.

For a current analysis of the difficulties of unlimited growth, see *Mankind at the Turning Point* by Mihajlo Mesarovic and Eduard Pestel (Dutton, Reader's Digest Press, New York, 1975); and *Human Ecology: Problems and Solutions* by Paul R. Ehrlich, Anne H. Ehrlich, and John P. Holdren (W. H. Freeman, San Francisco, 1973).

To note the sort of odd thought in the area of Western analyses of Eastern ideas, I need only read my mail. Herewith a typical letter, which I received while working on this manuscript:

> Dear Mr. Ornstein,
> The mystic experience is the birth experience experienced at an age when one is capable of using language. It is caused in either of two ways. That is by either too little oxygen—from breathing too slowly as when one is in a pensive state, or by a sudden deep breath as occurs when one is suddenly alarmed. Either experience recalls the birth breath, the shock of light and

cold, the first breath of life, the ecstasy of life which cannot be spoken of because the infant has no language. The mystic experience is the experience of life before language and after language. It is the beginning and the end, harmonizing in an inarticulate space of the brain. A humm. What else are we striving for when we strain our innermost consciences for the calming ecstasy of ohmm. I believe if you used a video-tape recording system while observing a person having a mystic experience in the instant replay you would be able to see the nimbus around the person. This is the birth energy—the first experience of light as recalled by the mystic. It is also the life force left after death.

I have done a deep study on this. Let me know if you want to speak to me about it.

2. Some Remarks on the
Evolutionary Background of Consciousness

I would highly recommend a reading of the original *Origin of Species,* by Darwin, and, for quite serious modern study, *Sociobiology,* by Edward Wilson (The Belknap Press of the Harvard University Press, Cambridge, 1975), although I must offer a caveat on the last chapter, concerning the extrapolation from insects to man.

I also recommend William James's *The Principles of Psychology* (Dover reprint of the original 1890 edition). James was a "functionalist," analyzing consciousness as an evolutionary organ of the mind.

The example on the "wisdom of the body" is from René Dubos's lecture at "Ways of Healing: Ancient and Modern," a conference co-sponsored by the University of California Medical Center, San Francisco, and The Institute for the Study of Human Knowledge, January 1976.

See also René Dubos, *Man Adapting* (Yale University Press, New Haven, 1965); Edward O. Wilson's article "Competitive and Aggressive Behavior" in *Man and Beast* (The Smithsonian Institution, Washington, D.C., 1971); Robert Heilbroner's *An Inquiry into the Human Prospect* (Norton, New York, 1974); and Shabistari's *The Secret Garden* (Dutton, New York, 1974).

3. A Cultural Hemianopia:
Intuition and Brain Structure

Professor Manfred Porkert's *Theoretical Foundations of Chinese Medicine* (The MIT Press, Cambridge, 1974) is a massive and groundbreaking work for Westerners interested in the conceptual world-view of an "Eastern Science."

For the ethic of sport as "transcendence," see George Leonard's *The Ultimate Athlete* (Viking, New York, 1975) and Michael Murphy's *Golf in the Kingdom* (Viking, New York, 1972).

I have covered much of the data on the two hemispheres of the brain in my *Psychology of Consciousness* (Viking, New York, 1973; Penguin, Baltimore, 1975) and in *The Nature of Human Consciousness* (Viking, New York, 1974, and W. H. Freeman, San Francisco, 1973).

4. On Psychiatroid Mentation and the Esoteric Traditions

The opening story is shortened slightly from Karl Menninger's "The Cinderella of Medicine," reprinted as Chapter 10 in *A Psychiatrist's World: The Selected Papers of Karl Menninger* (Viking, New York, 1959).

Sigmund Freud, in *Moses and Monotheism* (a Vintage reprint of the original 1939 edition), renews his reduction of religious approaches to neurotic processes. See, for instance, page 71:

> That conviction I acquired a quarter of a century ago, when I wrote my book on *Totem and Taboo* (in 1912), and it has only become stronger since. From then on I have never doubted that religious phenomena are to be understood only on the model of the neurotic symptoms of the individual, which are so familiar to us, as a return of long-forgotten important happenings in the primeval history of the human family, that they owe their obsessive character to that very origin and therefore derive their effect on mankind from the historical truth they contain. My uncertainty begins only at the point when I ask myself the question whether I have succeeded in proving this for the example of Jewish monotheism chosen here.

See Jerome Frank's *Persuasion and Healing* (Schocken Books, New York, 1975) for an overview, and E. Fuller Torrey's *The Death of Psychiatry* (Chilton, Radnor, Pa., 1974), for a savaging of the psychiatric discipline.

There are many useful reviews of psychotherapy, including Allen Bergin's "The Evaluation of Therapeutic Outcomes" in *Handbook of Psychotherapy and Behavior Change*, edited by Dr. Bergin with Sol L. Garfield (Wiley, New York, 1971). Dr. Bergin, along with co-author Hans Strupp, is responsible for another useful textbook on psychotherapy, *Changing Frontiers in the Science of Psychotherapy* (Aldine, Chicago, 1972).

See also Ernest G. Poser's article "The Effect of Therapists' Training on Group Therapeutic Outcome" in the *Journal of Consulting Psychology*, 1966, vol. 30, no. 4, pp. 283–289; Hans Eysenck's "The Effects of Psychotherapy" in the *International Journal of Psychiatry*, 1965, pp. 99–144; and David Malan's "The Outcome Problem in Psychotherapeutic Research" in the *Archives of General Psychiatry*, December 1973, vol. 29.

The status of psychotherapy as a science is coming under increasing legal challenge as well. See Bruce J. Ennis's and Thomas Litwack's "Psychiatry and the Presumption of Expertise: Flipping Coins in the Courtroom" in the *California Law Review*, vol. 62:671, pp. 694–752, 1975.

The story "Where It Starts" is from Idries Shah, *The Magic Monastery* (Dutton, New York, 1972).

5. The Believers and the Blind

The opening story is from Idries Shah's *Wisdom of the Idiots* (Dutton, New York, 1972).

These newspaper stories are from a collection I have published, *Common Knowledge* (Grossman/Viking, New York, 1975).

Several of the experiments described are summarized in Puthoff and Targ's 1974 paper in *Nature*, and in *Dream Telepathy*, by Montague Ullman, Stanley Krippner, and Allen Vaughn (Penguin, Baltimore, 1974).

For several extravagant statements, see "A Conversation with Stanley Krippner" in *Psychology Today*, October 1973.

6. A Lesson of Carlos Castaneda

Castaneda's *The Teachings of Don Juan: A Yaqui Way of Knowledge* (University of California Press, Berkeley, 1968), and *Journey to Ixtlan* (Simon and Schuster, New York, 1973) are useful. His other books are *A Separate Reality: Further Conversations with Don Juan* (Simon and Schuster, 1971) and *Tales of Power* (Simon and Schuster, 1974).

7. Caveat Meditator

There are innumerable proprietary publications on TM, as well as other popular books. I would not recommend any, but would merely note the extravagantly titled "Neurophysiology of Enlightenment," which is put out by their own organization, the MIU Press (Publication Number S.U. 7.).

Claudio Naranjo and I attempted to produce a survey of meditation techniques across cultures in *On the Psychology of Meditation* (Viking, New York, 1971).

For works by Gurdjieff's followers, see P. D. Ouspensky's *In Search of the Miraculous* (Harcourt, Brace, New York, 1949) and Maurice Nicoll's *The New Man* (Penguin, Baltimore, 1973). A charming memoir which avoids the cosmology and inflationism of Gurdjieff's disciples is Fritz Peters' *Boyhood with Gurdjieff* (Penguin, Baltimore, 1973). Perhaps the most fascinating and readable book on the subject is Rafael Lefort's *The Teachers of Gurdjieff* (Samuel Weiser, New York, 1973).

See David Pendlebury's selections from Sanai's *The Walled Garden* (Dutton, New York, 1976). The afterword is especially excellent.

The passage by Yakoub of Somnan that ends the chapter is entitled "Literature." It is from Idries Shah's *Thinkers of the East* (Penguin, Baltimore, 1972).

8. *A Spiritual Psychology for the Mainstream: Contemporary Sufism*

Shah's work makes available material not seen in the West for centuries. He has collected tales which are relevant to contemporary culture, in a usable form. I highlight his work as the most useful of the contemporary developments.

"The High Knowledge" is also from Shah's *Thinkers of the East*. "The Tale of the Sands" is from *Tales of the Dervishes* (Dutton, New York, 1970), as are "The Man with the Inexplicable Life" and "The Initiation of Malik Dinar."

"Unanswerable" and "How and What to Understand" are both from *Thinkers of the East*. That volume contains many stories on the difficulties in approach to traditional psychologies.

"The Man Who Was Easily Angered" is from *Tales of the Dervishes;* "Appetite" from *Thinkers of the East*.

"Meatballs" is from Shah's *The Magic Monastery*, as is "Duty."

"Contrary to Expectation" is from Shah's *The Book of the Book* (Octagon, New York, 1969). It provided much of the inspiration for this book as well.

Acknowledgments

I owe this book to those who have written to me about the practical problems arising from their interest in esoteric psychologies. I would like to thank Idries Shah for his generous permission to quote extensively from his stories. I would recommend that the reader interested in this book investigate Shah's writing. I should also thank those who raised interesting questions at symposia and seminars, often providing me with the many basic ideas of this book. I especially thank my friends David Sobel, Dan Okrent, Enoch Callaway, Dick Grossman, and Faith Hornbacher, and The Houston Astro Woman, whose conversation has inspired and encouraged me throughout.

(continued from page vi)